# יהוה

# What Is A Friend

By
תמר שרי ישראל

# יהוה

# What Is A Friend

They shall not hurt nor destroy in all my holy mountain: for the earth shall be full of the knowledge of the LORD יהוה , as the waters cover the sea. Isaiah 11:9 KJV

By תמר שרי ישראל

ISBN: 979-821860909-2

Editor: שראיה שרי ישראל

First hardcover edition, February 2025

Printed in the United States of America

# Table Of Contents

# Dedication

This book is dedicated to the spiritual resurrection of the righteous people of the Earth and to the establishment of the Kingdom of Shalom--the Kingdom of God, יהוה.

# Acknowledgement

I will forever thank my Father, יהוי for giving me the opportunity to put this book together. I pray every one of you reading this book has it in your hearts to want to learn, love and follow Abba יהוי. There is no greater love or blessing than his. May Abba יהוי guide you, protect you and keep you. I want you to know that יהוה loves you and if you love him you will do as John 14:15 KJV.

# Introduction

Shalom aleichem, I am excited to bring this knowledge to the forefront for your consideration. Have you ever asked yourself, is she my friend, is he my friend or are they my friends? Well, I promise you when it comes to יהוה (Yahweh), he definitely is a FRIEND. However, you will come to understand that He truly is your ONLY friend at the end of the day. Just to give you a little background about the Tetragrammaton, it is the four-letter Hebrew theonym יהוה (transliterated as YHWH), the name of God in the Hebrew Bible. The four letters, written and read from right to left (in Hebrew), are yodh, hay, waw, and hay. The scholarly consensus is that the original pronunciation of the Tetragrammaton was Yahweh (יהוה). A friend is someone you supposedly know well. A friend is someone you like a lot and is usually not a family member. Friends are supposed to provide support, fellowship, and often share mutual interests or experiences. Some people are such good friends that you begin to believe they are family. That's how close their bond is. Having a friend beyond 10 years is a blessing. I have personally seen people be friends for 20, 30, 40 years and longer! And no, these relationships I am referencing are not fake. Real relationships can be easy to recognize.

I employ you to be open minded while reading this book. I will give you some background information about my personal life experiences as well. First, please take into consideration this disclaimer. DISCLAIMER: This book is for educational purposes only. It is imperative that you do your own research. I am sharing my opinion from personal research and experience with no guarantee of gains or losses on investments, finance etc., just to be clear. This book is near and dear to my heart because it will entail certain parts of my childhood and adulthood life. Some of the things I write about, I am actually experiencing as I write this book. Some people had better life experiences than others. Nevertheless, I can say my upbringing was a challenge. I will share this piece of advice with you: sometimes Yahweh will test you in life with unfortunate situations. What's important is how you move forward afterwards. I am at a point in my life where I feel highly favored. I used to think that, if you had money to a certain extent, you could achieve more. Boy, was I wrong. It's the life experiences that make you rich through knowledge, wisdom, understanding, and time. I thank Yahweh for that.

# Preface

Before we dive into "what is a friend", let's look at some biblical scriptures that mention "friend, friends or friendship" found in the Torah. Let us look at scriptures outside the Torah as well, which can be found in the King James Version (**KJV**) Old Testament and New Testament.

See Case Law **§ 2 Samuel 16:17** KJV - "And Absalom said to Hushai, Is this thy kindness to thy friend? why wentest thou not with thy friend?"

See Case Law **§ Proverbs 6:3** KJV - "Do this now, my son, and deliver thyself, when thou art come into the hand of thy friend; go, humble thyself, and make sure thy friend."

See Case Law **§ Proverbs 27:10** KJV - "Thine own friend, and thy father's friend, forsake not; neither go into thy brother's house in the day of thy calamity: for better is a neighbour that is near than a brother far off."

See Case Law **§ Proverbs 17:17** KJV - "A friend loveth at all times, and a brother is born for adversity."

See Case Law **§ Job 6:27** KJV - "Yea, ye overwhelm the fatherless, and ye dig a pit for your friend."

See Case Law **§ Proverbs 17:18** KJV - "A man void of understanding striketh hands, and becometh surety in the presence of his friend."

See Case Law **§ Isaiah 41:8** KJV - "But thou, Israel, art my servant, Jacob whom I have chosen, the seed of Abraham my friend."

See Case Law **§ Proverbs 27:14** KJV - "He that blesseth his friend with a loud voice, rising early in the morning, it shall be counted a curse to him."

See Case Law **§ Psalms 35:14** KJV - "I behaved myself as though he had been my friend or brother: I bowed down heavily, as one that mourneth for his mother."

See Case Law **§ Psalms 41:9** KJV - "Yea, mine own familiar friend, in whom I trusted, which did eat of my bread, hath lifted up his heel against me."

See Case Law **§ Judges 14:20** KJV - "But Samson's wife was given to his companion, whom he had used as his friend."

See Case Law **§ Proverbs 27:9** KJV - "Ointment and perfume rejoice the heart: so doth the sweetness of a man's friend by hearty counsel."

See Case Law **§ Psalms 88:18** KJV - "Lover and friend hast thou put far from me, and mine acquaintance into darkness."

See Case Law **§ Song of Solomon 5:16** KJV - "His mouth is most sweet: yea, he is altogether lovely. This is my beloved, and this is my friend, O daughters of Jerusalem."

See Case Law § **Proverbs 19:6** KJV - "Many will intreat the favour of the prince: and every man is a friend to him that giveth gifts."

See Case Law § **Job 6:14** KJV - "To him that is afflicted pity should be shewed from his friend; but he forsaketh the fear of the Almighty."

See Case Law § **Proverbs 18:24** KJV - "A man that hath friends must shew himself friendly: and there is a friend that sticketh closer than a brother."

See Case Law § **Proverbs 6:1** KJV - "My son, if thou be surety for thy friend, if thou hast stricken thy hand with a stranger,"

See Case Law § **Proverbs 22:11** KJV - "He that loveth pureness of heart, for the grace of his lips the king shall be his friend."

See Case Law § **2 Samuel 15:37** KJV - "So Hushai David's friend came into the city, and Absalom came into Jerusalem."

See Case Law § **Proverbs 27:6** KJV - "Faithful are the wounds of a friend; but the kisses of an enemy are deceitful."

See Case Law § **Micah 7:5** KJV - "Trust ye not in a friend, put ye not confidence in a guide: keep the doors of thy mouth from her that lieth in thy bosom."

See Case Law § **2 Samuel 13:3** KJV - "But Amnon had a friend, whose name was Jonadab, the son of Shimeah David's brother: and Jonadab was a very subtil man."

See Case Law **§ Proverbs 27:17** KJV - "Iron sharpeneth iron; so a man sharpeneth the countenance of his friend."

See Case Law **§ 2 Chronicles 20:7** KJV - "Art not thou our God Yahweh, who didst drive out the inhabitants of this land before thy people Israel, and gavest it to the seed of Abraham thy friend for ever?"

See Case Law **§ Genesis 38:20** KJV - "And Judah sent the kid by the hand of his friend the Adullamite, to receive his pledge from the woman's hand: but he found her not."

See Case Law **§ Genesis 38:12** KJV - "And in process of time the daughter of Shuah Judah's wife died; and Judah was comforted, and went up unto his sheepshearers to Timnath, he and his friend Hirah the Adullamite."

See Case Law **§ Jeremiah 6:21** KJV - "Therefore thus saith the LORD Yahweh, Behold, I will lay stumblingblocks before this people, and the fathers and the sons together shall fall upon them; the neighbour and his friend shall perish."

See Case Law **§ Hosea 3:1** KJV - "Then said the LORD Yahweh unto me, Go yet, love a woman beloved of her friend, yet an adulteress, according to the love of the LORD Yahweh toward the children of Israel, who look to other gods, and love flagons of wine."

See Case Law § **Exodus 33:11** KJV - "And the LORD Yahweh spake unto Moses face to face, as a man speaketh unto his friend. And he turned again into the camp: but his servant Joshua, the son of Nun, a young man, departed not out of the tabernacle."

See Case Law § **Deuteronomy 13:6** KJV - "If thy brother, the son of thy mother, or thy son, or thy daughter, or the wife of thy bosom, or thy friend, which is as thine own soul, entice thee secretly, saying, Let us go and serve other gods, which thou hast not known, thou, nor thy fathers;"

See Case Law § **1 Kings 4:5** KJV - "And Azariah the son of Nathan was over the officers: and Zabud the son of Nathan was principal officer, and the king's friend:"

See Case Law § **2 Samuel 16:16** KJV - "And it came to pass, when Hushai the Archite, David's friend, was come unto Absalom, that Hushai said unto Absalom, God Yahweh save the king, God Yahweh save the king."

See Case Law § **Jeremiah 19:9** KJV - "And I will cause them to eat the flesh of their sons and the flesh of their daughters, and they shall eat every one the flesh of his friend in the siege and straitness, wherewith their enemies, and they that seek their lives, shall straiten them."

# Chapter 1

I was born in the Nation of Yahweh which was established in Miami, FL. I was honored to have been named by the honorable Yahweh Ben Yahweh. Growing up, I attended a private school through Yahweh's Education Center (YEC) which was located in Miami, FL. I cannot say I had "friends" as we referred to each other as Hebrew משפחה mashpacha (family). I honestly do not remember too much about my childhood unfortunately. My parents separated when I was 7 years old and me and my family relocated to Philadelphia, Pennsylvania. This is when things really started to take shape in my life. I learned some real hard life lessons growing up in Philly. I come from a large family of 11. I have 6 sisters and 5 brothers. I went to public school in Southwest Philadelphia and let me tell you, I experienced pure hell compared to YEC. I remember going home and telling my אמא emah (mum) about my bad experiences. I literally cried and told my emah not to send me back. I did not want to go back to public school. The children used filthy language, fought the teachers, the bathrooms were filthy, and there was recurring destruction to school property.

I was not used to this since I had just come from YEC. YEC was straight- up heaven (my opinion); a stress-free environment and a well-rounded respectable place to be. We were being taught at college level and there was no comparison to this education anywhere.

This scripture, see Case Law **§ Proverbs 18:24** KJV "A man that hath friends must shew himself friendly: and there is a friend that sticketh closer than a brother.", comes to mind because I remember being very friendly towards others but it was not reciprocated. Yes, rejection hurts. Let's be honest, when you put yourself out there and try to make new friends, it's not easy. Children can be mean unintentionally or deliberately. This may have something to do with their upbringing. According to Strong's Hebrew Concordance No. 7453, friend in Hebrew is pronounced ray-ah (רעה); it means an associate (more or less close):--brother, companion, fellow, friend, husband, lover, neighbour, × (an-)other. I always extended my friendship to others as this is what I was taught at YEC. But, sometimes people do not know how to take someone being kind to them. For example, they may wonder why you are being so nice to them. If you are not strong mentally, someone can try and make you feel like something is wrong with you. There is nothing wrong with showing love and kindness to others.

*Merriam-Webster* dictionary defines friend (noun) as: 1a: one attached to another by affection or esteem; b: acquaintance 2a: one that is not hostile; b: one that is of the same nation, party, or group; 3: one that favors or promotes something (such as a charity); 4: a favored companion; 5: Friend : a member of a Christian sect that stresses Inner Light, rejects sacraments and an ordained ministry, and opposes war called also Quaker; 6: a person included in a list of one's designated connections on a social media service. Verb: friended; friending; friends; 1: to act as the friend of : befriend. 2: to include (someone) in one's list of designated friends on a social media service.

Even when faced with adversity, you must keep moving forward. Showing yourself friendly does not mean being a fool. We all have an invisible bubble around ourselves and we tend to stay within that bubble too often, as it is our comfort zone. When I travel or find myself in unfamiliar places, I show myself friendly. Of course, you want to keep your eyes open and be aware of your surroundings. People tend to take better care of others who show themselves friendly versus someone downright unfriendly. People can be rude and disrespectful by being impolite, inconsiderate, or mean towards someone else. Simply put, sometimes people are just having a bad day or they are unconscious of their every action.

Ever come into contact with someone while you are out and about, and for no reason they are rude to you? How about being invited to an event and the individual who invited you acts like a jerk the entire time? I cannot tell you how many times my daughter got on my case for "letting someone mistreat me". I have learned, it is not worth it to try and get even with someone. Insecurity can cause someone to insult another human being for absolutely no reason. When someone needs to pull another person down for no reason, they obviously have issues within themselves. Have you ever had a friend throw jabs at you or indirectly insult you? Why can't we compliment one another and mean it in a nice way. Some people mean well, but their actions could push you away. People do not know just how much their actions have an effect on us. Fear causes people to act towards you in a mean way, and it's really because they lack understanding. Fear can cause people to become paranoid, anxious, judgemental, hateful, and even frightened. Like it or not, people tend to be judgemental whether they want to admit it or not. How we show ourselves to others will shape future relationships that will either blossom or decay. We, as spiritual beings, must show ourselves friendly. You might ask, how can one exhibit themself as friendly? We can do this by outwardly showing kindness, consideration, and via visible affirmative actions. I remember back in grammar school how I used to be so nice only to get my feelings hurt and there were times that it did bring tears to my eyes.

I would tell myself that I would be mean the next time. Nevertheless, why did I turn right back around and befriend the same children who hurt my feelings? Children can be like that sometimes, friends one day and enemies the next. Forgive but never forget! The scripture, see Case Law **§ Ruth 2:13** KJV - "Then she said, Let me find favour in thy sight, my lord; for that thou hast comforted me, and for that thou hast spoken friendly unto thine handmaid, though I be not like unto one of thine handmaidens." comes to mind when I think back to my childhood. We, as spiritual beings, often think of our friends and their friends as our own friends or acquaintances. I've learned that your friends and their friends are just that, friends with common likes and dislikes. It'd be nice if everyone could get along but sometimes that's just not the case. Children often repeat what they hear and see at home. Hence, you have your childhood friend that feels the need to boss everyone around and maybe even hit other children. No, not many would take kindly to this behavior. Would you consider someone like this a good friend? Probably not. How we speak to our friend says a lot about us as well. Did you know that a soft-spoken person can easily deliver bad news versus a plainspoken individual? I'm not sure if I agree with the saying that being rude is contagious. Just because someone was rude to you does not make it okay to go and do the same thing to another.

When you think of the word companion, what do you think? In my opinion, a companion is someone that is an associate, comrade, or someone that accompanies another. A companion can also be someone who is closely connected to someone else. A companion could be a friend, spouse, or neighbor. I moved around a lot as a child, so every time I made new friends; we packed up and moved again. That was not easy, let me tell you! After a while I became numb to the need to make friends. I mean, what was the point if I knew in 6 months time I would be moving again. After I left YEC, my life was never the same. I really began to understand what hell truly was. Imagine coming from a large family and still feeling alone. I was a tomboy so my sisters never paid attention to me. I hung out with my brothers and fit right in with them. I played football and basketball up till I could no longer play (became a teenager). I had a ball playing rough with the boys, no crying, or wimping was allowed! Growing up, I could not stand girls that were too girly, you know, the ones who are so prissy. Everything has to be pink, has to have sprinkles and glitter. Yuck! Turns out, I actually love pink now. Let's get back on topic. Though I was a tomboy growing up, I did have friends who were girly and I treated them equally or as good as anyone else. Some of them were nice to me and then you had some that were nasty.

I remember playing hooky in school while attending public school in southwest philadelphia for 3 days straight. Yes, my emah found out about it and you bet your rear end, I was disciplined rightfully so. When I was in the 3rd grade, this girl that I thought was my so-called friend taught me bad things. I learned a lot of bad things from public school. My emah forbade me from hanging out with her. I did not listen until it was too late. Sadly, it was time to walk away from that so-called friendship; we often fail at this part. From a very young age, I knew my walk in this life was different, see Case Law **§ Micah 4:5** KJV - "For all people will walk every one in the name of his god, and we will walk in the name of the LORD Yahweh our God for ever and ever." As a child I could never do the same things other children did. I did not celebrate birthdays, honor pagan festivities, carry out MAN-made customs and so-called traditions. We only honored Yahweh's High Holy days, see Case Law **§ Exodus 23:17** KJV - "Three times in the year all thy males shall appear before the Lord GOD Yahweh." We kept the shabbath, and there was no monkey business about it. When my parents separated, my emah did not stray from the teachings of Yahweh. I am following the same path, my children will only learn of Yahweh, their history, language, land and names. When I lived in Philadelphia, I was surrounded by culturally diverse people. I cannot say that about the South, meaning Florida. People up north tend to be more open minded from my experiences anyway.

I don't know if I can say a child has enough experience to make a rational judgement (to an extent) whether someone is a good friend or not. I could tell when someone was being kind to me and when they were just being unfriendly. See Case Law § **Job 16:20** KJV - "My friends scorn me: but mine eye poureth out tears unto God Yahweh." We tend to take someone's word at face value when we are children. Words do hurt and we should be careful about what we say. I do not know anyone who probably has not shed a tear because of mean things being said to them as a child. When someone scorns you, they dislike and disrespect you. They display signs of mockery, often combined with indignation. The teased individual may also experience being laughed at or ridiculed. Signs that you are being scorned include: mockery; joke, laughingstock, mark, target, butt, scoff, and sport just to name a few. This scripture came to mind, see Case Law § **Job 19:19** KJV - "All my inward friends abhorred me: and they whom I loved are turned against me." Experience truly is the best teacher. Our childhood does ultimately play a huge role in who we become and what we do with our life. Some people grow up in well-established families and do absolutely nothing with their lives. Then you have people who grew up less fortunate; who actually make a difference in the world. I think it is a good idea that we find ways to contribute to society where we can make a difference.

See Case Law **§ Job 19:14** KJV - "My kinsfolk have failed, and my familiar friends have forgotten me." Trying to explain to your family your state of mind as a child is taken as a joke. How many people take children seriously? Even when my children come and tell me things I give them a certain look. Children tend to exaggerate things a bit. I cannot think of a situation where I did this to my parents (they may tell a different story). Nevertheless, my childhood wasn't the best but it also wasn't the worst. I have good and bad memories. I moved around a lot as a child after leaving YEC, so my childhood friends are not many. You'd think it would be easier to make friends, but kindness often goes unnoticed. See Case Law **§ Judges 8:35** KJV - "Neither shewed they kindness to the house of Jerubbaal, namely, Gideon, according to all the goodness which he had shewed unto Israel." See Case Law **§ Psalms 117:2** KJV - "For his merciful kindness is great toward us: and the truth of the LORD Yahweh endureth for ever. Praise ye the LORD Yahweh." Most of us have likely experienced that "bend over backwards" kind of kindness that, to be honest, makes people a little uncomfortable. I found myself going out of my way to be kind to others and it is not appreciated. See Case Law **§ 1 Samuel 20:15** KJV - "But also thou shalt not cut off thy kindness from my house for ever: no, not when the LORD Yahweh hath cut off the enemies of David every one from the face of the earth."

Yahweh teaches us to be kind to others, we are to want for our Hebrew brothers and sisters what we want for ourselves. Including a bowl of soup (figuratively speaking). See Case Law § **Leviticus 19:34** KJV - "But the stranger that dwelleth with you shall be unto you as one born among you, and thou shalt love him as thyself; for ye were strangers in the land of Egypt: I am the LORD Yahweh your God." To show kindness is to be of a gentle, affectionate, thoughtful, attentive, sympathetic or helpful nature. If you know anyone with these characteristics, count your blessings. See Case Law § **Job 42:10** KJV - "And the LORD Yahweh turned the captivity of Job, when he prayed for his friends: also the LORD Yahweh gave Job twice as much as he had before." The blessing of a good friend is more than the "be with you" variety. Rather than hand you the shirt off their back, they'll make sure that both of your needs are met so that neither one of you are lacking the most basic of necessities. Yahweh truly is the greatest friend I will ever have, he surpasses all of these qualifications and then some. He is the Creator, after all. There are people who have similar characteristics but they are not many in number. See Case Law § **Ecclesiastiscus 6:17** KJV - "Whoso feareth the Lord Yahweh shall direct his friendship aright: for as he is, so shall his neighbour be also." Another quality of a good friend is that they will let you know when you hurt them. They let you know if you are confusing them, or if they see you doing something unwise, and they can tell when you're concealing your true self.

See Case Law **§ Proverbs 22:24** KJV - "Make no friendship with an angry man; and with a furious man thou shalt not go:" The Bible gives us much wisdom and knowledge. The dictionary gives us understanding. As a child, I did not study my name as I do now. I used to hate my name because public school teachers would poke fun at my name. And to top it off, my emah always called me over my other siblings; so you can imagine the height of irritation (I can laugh about it now). I attended a magnet art middle school in Liberty City, Miami, Florida. Every year on the last day of school I remember an entourage of cops would be there because of some kind of threat. It was nerve- wrecking, so I always got permission from my emah to ditch the last day of school. When I started junior high in Upper Darby Pennsylvania (Have I mentioned I moved around a lot?), that's when I got a better feel of true friendship. I specifically had two female friends who were like Bonnie and Clyde. We did everything together, shopping, roller skating, sleepovers; I was really starting to see my life turn around. Reminds me of, see Case Law **§ Proverbs 17:17** KJV - "A friend loveth at all times, and a brother is born for adversity." As I was going through adolescence, I saw how Yahweh blessed me with qualifying characteristics of what a good friend could be. Long story short, I relocated to Delaware and, yes, I made friends there as well. Once I started high school, I knew exactly what kind of person I wanted to be and who I wanted to hang out with.

What I did not know was that this would be the very last school where I did make friends. I witnessed people be friends one minute and the next it was over. Some friendships ended over a boy, some friendships ended over lies, and some friendships ended because they outgrew one another. What I did not understand was why would anyone let something happen to their friendship especially if the issue is so small and meaningless. This came to mind, see Case Law **§ Psalms 35:14** KJV - "I behaved myself as though he had been my friend or brother: I bowed down heavily, as one that mourneth for his mother." Time and time again, Yahweh always had a stable place in my heart. Yahweh is always available when I need someone to talk to. Yahweh is there when you need Him. I cannot say that about any of my friends. Yahweh will be a better friend to you than any other being. He is just, good, kind, loving, and merciful. See Case Law **§ Psalms 108:12** KJV - "Give us help from trouble: for vain is the help of man." See Case Law **§ Psalms 121:2** KJV - "My help cometh from the LORD Yahweh, which made heaven and earth." I learned the hard way, not to put trust in man, see Case Law **§ Psalms 146:3** KJV - "Put not your trust in princes, nor in the son of man, in whom there is no help." Too many times have I been let down. Too many times have I been lied to. See Case Law **§ Psalms 115:9** KJV - "O Israel, trust thou in the LORD Yahweh: he is their help and their shield."

My experiences with friends in high school were good. By this time I knew exactly what was acceptable and what was not. See Case Law **§ Psalms 46:5** KJV - "God Yahweh is in the midst of her; she shall not be moved: God Yahweh shall help her, and that right early." Something else to consider, see Case Law **§ Isaiah 50:9** KJV - "Behold, the Lord GOD Yahweh will help me; who is he that shall condemn me? lo, they all shall wax old as a garment; the moth shall eat them up." See Case Law **§ Psalms 40:17** KJV - "But I am poor and needy; yet the Lord Yahweh thinketh upon me: thou art my help and my deliverer; make no tarrying, O my God Yahweh." I attended night school in Philadelphia, though I graduated from high school with my classmates. They never saw me in actuality. That's the perk of going to night school. People can present themselves as though they are friendly, when they really are snakes. Tone says a lot about an individual. You can tell if someone is being nice or just playing it safe to get what they want. See Case Law **§ Psalms 140:3** KJV - "They have sharpened their tongues like a serpent; adders' poison is under their lips. Selah." Talk is cheap especially if nothing good will come from it, see Case Law **§ Ecclesiastes 10:11** KJV - "Surely the serpent will bite without enchantment; and a babbler is no better." According to Strong's Hebrew Concordance No. 5175, serpent in Hebrew is Nachash (נחש); verb, it is the act of divination or seeking omens. It is used in the context of attempting to gain insight or foretell future events through supernatural means.

This practice is often associated with pagan rituals and is explicitly condemned in the Hebrew Scriptures as contrary to the worship and reliance on the one true God Yahweh. Nachash, a primitive root; properly, to hiss, i.e. Whisper a (magic) spell; generally, to prognosticate -- X certainly, divine, enchanter, (use) X enchantment, learn by experience, X indeed, diligently observe. So, when you are dealing with someone who exudes these behaviors, you know exactly who they are. In ancient Northeast Africa, divination was a familiar practice among various cultures, including the Canaanites, Egyptians, and Babylonians. It involved clarifying signs, omens, or using objects like arrows, entrails, or celestial bodies to predict the future or gain guidance. Hebrew Israelites were schooled to avoid such practices, as they were seen as relying on powers other than Yahweh. The Laws of יהוה unmistakably forbids astrology in passages such as, see Case Law **§ Deuteronomy 18:10-12** KJV, emphasizing the importance of seeking guidance from Yahweh alone. Believe it or not, people use enchantment to their advantage or so they think. Yahweh knows all. Ever wonder how certain individuals luck up from certain business ventures or contracts that are considered out of this world. The use of spells, the art or act of enchanting is an abomination to Yahweh. Some people gain relationships with enchantments, you may not know it but they do (pray about it).

See Case Law **§ Genesis 3:13** KJV - "And the LORD God Yahweh said unto the woman, What is this that thou hast done? And the woman said, The serpent beguiled me, and I did eat." Just because someone presents themselves as a potential mate, whether platonic or not, you need to use caution. If something looks good, it does not mean it is good for you. I know you are familiar with what a hex is? Charm is another enchantment; so is glamour. All over the world things are dangled right before you to entice you or lure you in. At YEC, I learned about Yahweh's 28 moral behavioral attributes: righteous, just, upright, honest, straightforward, open, honorable, good, excellent, well-behaved, right conduct, principle, ethical, truth, right, rule, teachings, conform, virtuous, chaste, action, mind, feelings, Will, character, nature, judgement and caution. These are characteristics of Yahweh, god-like qualities that we all should exude and look for in each other. See Case Law **§ Ezekiel 3:21** KJV - "Nevertheless if thou warn the righteous man, that the righteous sin not, and he doth not sin, he shall surely live, because he is warned; also thou hast delivered thy soul." I have learned not to fling the word "friend" around too loosely nowadays. You can think you know someone for 10 years and in a blink of an eye, they switch up on you. We know for a fact that Yahweh does not operate that way. See Case Law **§ Psalms 119:164** KJV - "Seven times a day do I praise thee because of thy righteous judgments."

See Case Law § **Psalms 97:12** KJV - "Rejoice in the LORD Yahweh, ye righteous; and give thanks at the remembrance of his holiness." Once I completed high school, I attended college and made acquaintances with my fellow classmates. I barely had time for socialization, but my experiences with others never fell short. My main goal was to complete my school work and keep my head low. I did just that. As I entered adulthood, I really did not understand exactly how I would reach my goals. I just knew I had to achieve them somehow. Friends came and went. Distractions are like luck, they are both forces outside of our control. It's almost as if someone put blinders on your eyes so you don't know which direction to take. See Case Law § **Psalms 37:32** KJV - "The wicked watcheth the righteous, and seeketh to slay him." Unfortunately, some so-called friends will go out of their way to try and sabotage you. Yahweh sees all of it. See Case Law § **Proverbs 11:30** KJV - "The fruit of the righteous is a tree of life; and he that winneth souls is wise." Knowing who you are helps to create amazing bonds with others. Good friends are not trying to copy you, they are accomplished themselves. See Case Law § **Proverbs 10:21** KJV - "The lips of the righteous feed many: but fools die for want of wisdom." I have seen how some friends mean good. If only their intentions were as sweet as their words. See Case Law § **Proverbs 18:10** KJV - "The name of the LORD Yahweh is a strong tower: the righteous runneth into it, and is safe."

# Chapter 2

What is a good friend? According to Strong's Hebrew Concordance No. 2895; verb, the Hebrew word for good is *towb* (טוב). In ancient Hebrew knowledge, the concept of "*towb*" was wholly fused with the understanding of Yahweh's creation and His moral standards. The word is notoriously used in the creation narrative in Genesis, where Yahweh repeatedly proclaims His creation as good. This mirrors the intrinsic value and orderliness that Yahweh infused in the world. In the context of Hebrew Israelite society, towb also encircled the idea of collective well-being and ethical living according to Yahweh"s commandments. Towb is a primitive root, to be (transitively, do or make) good (or well) in the widest sense -- be (do) better, cheer, be (do, seem) good, (make) goodly, X please, (be, do, go, play) well. See Case Law **§ Psalms 119:68** KJV - "Thou art good, and doest good; teach me thy statutes." A friend is honest, true to self, outgoing and has many other good qualities.

See Case Law **§ Isaiah 52:7** KJV - "How beautiful upon the mountains are the feet of him that bringeth good tidings, that publisheth peace; that bringeth good tidings of good, that publisheth salvation; that saith unto Zion, Thy God Yahweh reigneth!" Good friends are bold in that they like to do things, consider things, feel things, and share those things with you. You may be wondering, "How does Yahweh fit into this scenario"? Yahweh can do things your good friends cannot. He is sovereign, all-knowing, all-being, omnipresent and able to carry out tasks we only could dream of. Yahweh is all powerful. See Case Law **§ Deuteronomy 6:18** KJV - "And thou shalt do that which is right and good in the sight of the LORD Yahweh: that it may be well with thee, and that thou mayest go in and possess the good land which the LORD Yahweh sware unto thy fathers". We live our lives as though we are in charge when in fact Yahweh has the last say. Yahweh is an awesome friend, He will never lie to us. He will tell us straight to our face. See Case Law **§ Deuteronomy 7:10** KJV - "And repayeth them that hate him to their face, to destroy them: he will not be slack to him that hateth him, he will repay him to his face." Real friends should be upfront with you no matter what. It is ethical to be honest with one another. See Case Law **§ Deuteronomy 5:6** KJV - "The LORD Yahweh talked with you face to face in the mount out of the midst of the fire,"

See Case Law **§ Psalms 34:16** KJV - "The face of the LORD Yahweh is against them that do evil, to cut off the remembrance of them from the earth."

Some of my friends are very straightforward, even when I do not want to hear it. If you really want to learn from a genuine friendship that is historical in text, check out Yahweh's relationship with Abraham. See Case Law **§ Genesis 18:19** KJV - "For I know him, that he will command his children and his household after him, and they shall keep the way of the LORD Yahweh, to do justice and judgment; that the LORD Yahweh may bring upon Abraham that which he hath spoken of him." The world is a serious place, but the non-stop antics can make being taken seriously quite difficult. And while visions, goals, and attitudes are often comparable, even the best reciprocal friendships know there are times when each person must pull away to reflect and renew on their own. Yahweh, our heavenly father knows us all better than anyone ever could. Your deepest desires, ambitions, wants, needs, thoughts, are all known to Him and not hidden. See Case Law **§ Ecclesiasticus 6:7** KJV - "If thou wouldest get a friend, prove him first and be not hasty to credit him." Yahweh is a great example of a true friend. It is a mission Yahweh takes upon Himself when it comes to protecting you. He will do it from now on to eternity. Whether ending relationships current or not, shielding you from impending harm, or even at times protecting you from yourself. There are people we can trust to an extent. Untrustworthy people don't make good friends. We believe our good friends to be solid people.

If not, remove them. See Case Law § **Micah 7:5** KJV - "Trust ye not in a friend, put ye not confidence in a guide: keep the doors of thy mouth from her that lieth in thy bosom." Yahweh has compassion and empathy unlike any other, which makes Him a wonderful friend. See Case Law § **Isaiah 41:8** KJV - "But thou, Israel, art my servant, Jacob whom I have chosen, the seed of Abraham my friend." No one can offer you better protection than Yahweh. Our heavenly Father Yahweh listens to our hopes, fears, questions, dreams, foolishness, musings, prattlings, and more, not out of need, but because He genuinely cares. Have you ever asked yourself if someone was a friend or enemy? Well, Yahweh definitely is a friend. The definition of hostile is, of or relating to an enemy, marked by malevolence : having or showing unfriendly feelings. Someone who is openly opposed or resisting, not hospitable. Having an intimidating, antagonistic, or offensive nature. Do not expect to attract and receive promising, generous, or friendly welcome from this sort of person. A hostile individual will not be readily receptive. Hostile in the Strong's Hebrew Concordance No. 7136 is Qarah (קארה), verb: a primitive root; to light upon (chiefly by accident); causatively, to bring about; specifically, to impose timbers (for roof or floor) -- appoint, lay (make) beams, befall, bring, come (to pass unto), floor, (hap) was, happen (unto), meet, send good speed. Yahweh is not hostile unless you give Him a reason to be.

In ancient northeast Africa, the relationship between Yahweh and His people was often seen as a contractual agreement, with blessings for submission and curses for defiance. The term qarah reflects the offence of this contractual obligation, where Hebrew Israelites' actions are contrary to the anticipation established by Yahweh. This notion is absolutely embedded in the contractual doctrine of the Old Testament, where devotion to Yahweh is paramount for the people's well-being. Thus, we know that Yahweh is again a true friend because he will not be hostile to you unless given a reason to be. See Case Law **§ Psalms 41:9** KJV - "Yea, mine own familiar friend, in whom I trusted, which did eat of my bread, hath lifted up his heel against me." Once you decide to start and build a relationship with Yahweh, you will come to learn that He will become your favored companion. See Case Law **§ 2 Chronicles 20:12** KJV - "O our Yahweh, wilt thou not judge them? for we have no might against this great company that cometh against us; neither know we what to do: but our eyes are upon thee." No friend will show you favor nor promote you the way Yahweh can. To regard or treat with favor: to do a kindness for, to treat gently or carefully, to show partiality toward, to give support or confirmation to; to afford advantages for success are just a few benefits of Yahweh's favor over you.

See Case Law **§ Proverbs 22:1** KJV - "A good name is rather to be chosen than great riches, and loving favour rather than silver and gold." To act as the friend of. This is how Yahweh returns His love and care for you. He acts as a friend. See Case Law **§ Proverbs 8:35** KJV - "For whoso findeth me findeth life, and shall obtain favour of the LORD Yahweh." Too many people forget that there's ONE MAN in Charge and His name is YAHWEH, see Case Law **§ Proverbs 29:26** KJV - "Many seek the ruler's favour; but every man's judgment cometh from the LORD Yahweh." Building a sound relationship with Yahweh starts with knowledge. When you get to know someone you learn things about them. Like, what they like and do not like for example. See Case Law **§ Psalms 92:5** KJV - "O LORD Yahweh, how great are thy works! and thy thoughts are very deep." Yahweh already knows everything about you, but we do not know everything about Him. See Case Law **§ Isaiah 55:8** KJV - "For my thoughts are not your thoughts, neither are your ways my ways, saith the LORD Yahweh." See Case Law **§ Proverbs 16:3** KJV - "Commit thy works unto the LORD Yahweh, and thy thoughts shall be established." We can learn how Yahweh wants us to be. See Case Law **§ Ecclesiastes 12:13** KJV - "Let us hear the conclusion of the whole matter: Fear Yahweh, and keep his commandments: for *this is* the whole *duty* of man."

A friend lets you get to know them personally. This is what Yahweh does. When you are ready to seek him out, Yahweh will place it on your heart to want to get to know Him personally. Trust me, you will go out of your way to learn about Yahweh. To connect with Him and you'll want to be friends with Him. The kingdom of Shalom, the kingdom of Yahweh is at hand, it truly is.

See Case Law **§ Joel 2:1** KJV - "Blow ye the trumpet in Zion, and sound an alarm in my holy mountain: let all the inhabitants of the land tremble: for the day of the LORD Yahweh cometh, for it is nigh at hand;" Only Yahweh can cause you to know firsthand how He truly is a REAL friend. A native who is friendly to settlers or invaders, that's Yahweh. He created the air we breathe, the food we eat, the land we walk on, and much more. See Case Law **§ Revelation 4:11** KJV - "Thou art worthy, O Lord Yahweh, to receive glory and honour and power: for thou hast created all things, and for thy pleasure they are and were created." See Case Law **§ Isaiah 45:18** KJV - "For thus saith the LORD Yahweh that created the heavens; Yahweh himself that formed the earth and made it; he hath established it, he created it not in vain, he formed it to be inhabited: I am the LORD Yahweh; and there is none else." Yahweh is a kind of friend that will provide you with what is useful or necessary in achieving an end. Ever been in a situation where you needed help to fight an adversary?

Or where you have been in a situation where a so-called friend needed your help? Yahweh was definitely aiding you as a friend in your time of need. Yahweh is all-knowing. He is the one to whom secrets are confessed. It's possible that a best friend can slip up and tell your darkest secrets. Yahweh truly does know all. See Case Law § **Psalms 90:8** KJV - "Thou hast set our iniquities before thee, our secret sins in the light of thy countenance." See Case Law § **Psalms 25:14** KJV - "The secret of the LORD Yahweh is with them that fear him; and he will shew them his covenant." See Case Law § **Ecclesiastes 12:14** KJV - "For Yahweh shall bring every work into judgment, with every secret thing, whether it be good, or whether it be evil." A good friend is open and intimate with you. This is something Yahweh does with the people who seek Him out and want to have a relationship with Him. Intimate means, marked by a warm friendship developing through long association. It is not wise to only be friends with Yahweh just because you know He comes with benefits. Too many people are only friends with others for: financial gains, social networking gains, political gains; you name it. Yahweh wants us to be in a state of devotion at all times, not just when we need him. That means be grateful for the good and bad, and stay in a grateful state of mind. See Case Law § **Isaiah 45:19** KJV - "I have not spoken in secret, in a dark place of the earth: I said not unto the seed of Jacob, Seek ye me in vain: I the LORD Yahweh speak righteousness, I declare things that are right."

See Case Law **§ Deuteronomy 4:5** KJV - "But if from thence thou shalt seek the LORD Yahweh thy God, thou shalt find him, if thou seek him with all thy heart and with all thy soul." When Yahweh is your friend I can guarantee that He is engaged with you. There is nothing you will lack. Yahweh will see to it that all your needs are met. See Case Law **§ Psalms 34:10** KJV - "The young lions do lack, and suffer hunger: but they that seek the LORD Yahweh shall not want any good thing." To experience a very personal or private nature with Yahweh is intimacy. These are characteristics that a true friend should have. I am sure we can all agree that Yahweh is a very close friend or confidant: an intimate friend. Yahweh will always have your back if ever you are in trouble and need Him. Let me be clear about this, you must be righteous in His sight. If we are being honest with ourselves, why should He protect an evil doer? See Case Law **§ Proverbs 28:27** KJV - "He that giveth unto the poor shall not lack: but he that hideth his eyes shall have many a curse." Yahweh is the kind of friend that will send you warnings. See Case Law **§ Ezekiel 3:21** KJV - "Nevertheless if thou warn the righteous man, that the righteous sin not, and he doth not sin, he shall surely live, because he is warned; also thou hast delivered thy soul." We, the righteous people of the Earth, must walk upright before Yahweh.

See Case Law **§ Proverbs 2:7** KJV - "He layeth up sound wisdom for the righteous: he is a buckler to them that walk uprightly." We know Yahweh's affection for us when we feel cared for, and that fondness is present. Nobody other than Yahweh can give you such a powerful feeling or emotion. A feeling that just brings tears to your eyes, especially when you get deep in thought about just how good Yahweh is to us. See Case Law **§ Proverbs 10:21** KJV - "The lips of the righteous feed many: but fools die for want of wisdom." When someone inclines themself to you, it's as if you have their undivided attention. To know that Yahweh will perform this is mindblowing. Yahweh actually favors you. What a wonderful thing to know and believe. See Case Law **§ Psalms 17:6** KJV - "I have called upon thee, for thou wilt hear me, O Yahweh: incline thine ear unto me, and hear my speech." To have favorable regard is amazing. A friend is one that is of the same nation, crew, or category. We know Yahweh is a righteous man. Thus, He fits this description. See Case Law **§ Proverbs 8:35** KJV - "For whoso findeth me findeth life, and shall obtain favour of the LORD Yahweh." I do not think there is a friend like Yahweh; a man who is able to truly support you. To be fully able to endure whatever it is you are going through bravely or quietly. How many times have you promoted the interests or cause of a so-called friend? Was the favor returned? Well, with Yahweh He will always support, bear, sustain, help, and advocate for you.

I cannot say that about too many so-called friends in my life currently. Yahweh is truly supporting me, through thick and thin. See Case Law § **Proverbs 3:4** KJV - "So shalt thou find favour and good understanding in the sight of Yahweh and man." Typically when we run into legal matters, we look for an attorney. Yahweh is an advocate for you. He will uphold or defend you and your cause as valid or right. It takes real power to do this. Man is not capable of performing these miracles. Ever had a friend argue over something tied to you? Or argue for you? Yahweh will definitely argue or vote for you and you will see results. A relationship with a true friend oftentimes involves assisting one another. Now, let's be honest. Some so-called friends are poor at being there when you really need them. Yahweh is a thorough kind of friend. He does not put on a show of acting like he's helping you like some people. He actually will help someone, give assistance. See Case Law § **Psalms 121:2** KJV - "My help cometh from the LORD Yahweh, which made heaven and earth." When I was on multiple social media platforms, I remember asking some of my so-called friends if they could share my posts. Something that cost nothing out of their pockets. All I received were crickets. But when they had a business idea, product or service they sure asked me to do it and like a good friend, I complied. See, this I testify to you today and forever more that Yahweh is God and a real friend.

See Case Law § **Psalms 146:3** KJV - "Put not your trust in princes, nor in the son of man, in whom there is no help." See Case Law § **Psalms 115:9** KJV - "O Israel, trust thou in the LORD Yahweh: he is their help and their shield." Sometimes people can get jealous of your achievements. Now, Yahweh will get jealous if you give worship to false gods because Yahweh is the one and only CREATOR. See Case Law § **Exodus 20:5** KJV - "Thou shalt not bow down thyself to them, nor serve them: for I the LORD Yahweh thy God am a jealous God Yahweh, visiting the iniquity of the fathers upon the children unto the third and fourth generation of them that hate me;" When situations are made more pleasant or bearable, know that this is help from Yahweh's doings. This is a form of help from Yahweh alone. The only person capable of rescuing you from any and all problems is Yahweh. Sometimes our so-called friends come through when we need them and sometimes they do not. I hope you understand and know that only Yahweh can save you. See Case Law § **Deuteronomy 4:39** KJV - "Know therefore this day, and consider it in thine heart, that the LORD Yahweh he is God in heaven above, and upon the earth beneath: there is none else." See Case Law § **Deuteronomy 20:4** KJV - "For the LORD Yahweh your God is he that goeth with you, to fight for you against your enemies, to save you."

The benefits of Yahweh coming to your aid is underrated. The advantages of having Yahweh as your friend produces good and helpful results or effects. This can help promote your overall well-being. See Case Law § **Isaiah 45:5** KJV - "I am the LORD Yahweh, and there is none else, there is no God beside me: I girded thee, though thou hast not known me:" In life, we sometimes hit a bumpy road and experience hardships. It would be wise to include Yahweh in every aspect of your life. After all, He created everything. Financial help from Yahweh can come in any shape or form. For example, a total stranger randomly pays for your groceries when you least expect it. It could come in the form of a surprise bonus from your employer, lottery ticket, or just random situations to fulfill your needs. See Case Law § **Ecclesiastes 10:19** KJV - "A feast is made for laughter, and wine maketh merry: but money answereth all things." Some of us have had to rely on a so-called friend financially. Yahweh provides for you and has your back at every turn. Here's where things go wrong: a so-called friend is only around for self- gain. Pray that Yahweh places a hedge of protection over you and only allows righteous people to come your way.

An act of kindness is what you will likely experience with Yahweh as your companion. I want to be straightforward, open and honest. With Yahweh as your friend, you will have quite an advantage. Have you ever experienced a time in your life where everything just fell in place in a day? Genesis 39:3 KJV - "And his master saw that the LORD Yahweh was with him, and that the LORD Yahweh made all that he did to prosper in his hand." How many people do you know that would genuinely help you get where you want to be? I know Yahweh as one of them. Not only does Yahweh help you go where you want to be in life, He also advances you unlike any other. Could you use some help promoting your business, or to negotiate better pay? Yahweh can promote you to where the entire world will recognize you, respect you and accept you. What a great boost to your personal achievements. According to Strong's Hebrew Concordance No. 6743 prosper in Hebrew is tsalach (צלאח), verb: or tsaleach {tsaw-lay'-akh}; a primitive root; to push forward, in various senses (literal or figurative, transitive or intransitive) -- break out, come (mightily), go over, be good, be meet, be profitable, (cause to, effect, make to, send) prosper(-ity, -ous, - ously). See Case Law § **Deuteronomy 29:9** KJV - "Keep therefore the words of this covenant, and do them, that ye may prosper in all that ye do."

In old Hebrew Israelite society, wealth and success were often seen as signs of Yahweh's favor and blessing. The idea of tsalach is deeply embedded in the contractual agreement between Yahweh and His people, where adherence to Yahweh's commandments was believed to lead to success. This understanding is mirrored in the broader old Eastern climate, where success was often attributed to the favor of the gods. To be ranked in a high position of authority, or given honor is Yahweh's way of raising you up. This is more proof of just how good of a friend Yahweh is. Allow me to ask you some questions that hopefully will make you reconsider some things. Have any of your friends contributed to the growth or prosperity of you? What about if a friend helped bring (something, such as an enterprise) into being? Or has any of your friends given you a start with the launch of a business or fund drive? For someone to do any of these things and then some would be rare. There is only one person in existence who truly wants to see you succeed and His name is Yahweh. With the right support and help from Yahweh there's nothing you cannot accomplish. See Case Law **§ Isaiah 54:17** KJV - "No weapon that is formed against thee shall prosper; and every tongue that shall rise against thee in judgment thou shalt condemn. This is the heritage of the servants of the LORD Yahweh, and their righteousness is of me, saith the LORD Yahweh."

Sometimes we don't know where to start but Yahweh can cause or facilitate the beginning of your dream whatever that may be. Thus, Yahweh will have you set going in the right direction. There's a saying, if you take the first step, Yahweh will take the next step. Generally speaking, when we want to start a new project, we must take action to start. I have learned nothing is a coincidence. Yahweh can cause you to experience a rapid rise in activity, growth, or popularity. I mean the benefits with Yahweh are unlimited and truly a blessing right before your eyes. That new business opportunity you were working on could take off or that new product you just created could fly off the shelves from massive sales! Yes, Yahweh can do all of this and more for you as your friend. You have to keep in mind that Yahweh is the Almighty Creator. He owns everything literally. So, who wouldn't want to be on good terms with Him? See Case Law **§ 1 Kings 8:60** KJV - "That all the people of the earth may know that the LORD Yahweh is God, and that there is none else." Wouldn't you want the right person guiding you in the right direction? I want to be on Yahweh's side and only HIS. See Case Law **§ Joshua 24:15** KJV - "And if it seem evil unto you to serve the LORD Yahweh, choose you this day whom ye will serve; whether the gods which your fathers served that were on the other side of the flood, or the gods of the Amorites, in whose land ye dwell: but as for me and my house, we will serve the LORD Yahweh."

No one can change you but there is one person who can change your heart. Only Yahweh can cause you to change for the better. This is another form of help from Yahweh, believe it or not. Not many friends are a good source of aid, but Yahweh is (this is my opinion, of course). Many people seek validation in the world. Seeking validation through Yahweh is a wise decision. We tend to forget that it is Yahweh who corroborates with others to vindicate us. See Case Law **§ 1 Samuel 16:13** KJV - "Then Samuel took the horn of oil, and anointed him in the midst of his brethren: and the Spirit of the LORD Yahweh came upon David from that day forward. So Samuel rose up, and went to Ramah." Help does come at a cost, however. Yahweh is more than able to carry this financial load. To keep in an existing state (as of repair, efficiency, or validity) : preserve from failure or decline; Yahweh is able. The Creator Yahweh is more than able to sustain you against opposition or danger : uphold and defend. To persevere in life is all possible with Yahweh. Only Yahweh can open doors no other man can and only Yahweh can close doors that no other man can open. See Case Law **§ Revelation 3:8** KJV - "I know thy works: behold, I have set before thee an open door, and no man can shut it: for thou hast a little strength, and hast kept my word, and hast not denied my name."

# Chapter 3

Life comes with challenges, especially when we deal with people of different backgrounds, cultures, and beliefs systems, etc. One thing you definitely need to pay attention to is who you call your friend. Unfortunately, not everyone means well, see Case Law **§ Proverb 1:16** KJV - "For their feet run to evil, and make haste to shed blood." This chapter is a warning to those of you with kind hearts, to use caution before you invite someone into your life and family. For someone to intentionally deceive another human being is wicked. Let's call it for what it is. I am not one to sugarcoat anything. Have you ever experienced someone seeking to injure, overthrow, or confound you? If so, you may have likely met one of your enemies. See Case Law **§ Proverbs 27:6** KJV - "Faithful are the wounds of a friend; but the kisses of an enemy are deceitful." I had these so-called friends in my life for years until Yahweh caused me to become aware of the little games they liked to play. It's tempting to state, "Wow, we've been through so much together".

I have known people since my childhood and some of them are like family to me. On the other hand, some who once were considered my friends have since been let go. Sometimes we can be very naive about people and their intentions. I regret that it took me so long to see that some people are not truly genuine or sincere. We create soul-ties when we have longterm relationships. It makes it much more challenging to let these so-called friends go. Think about it, if you have known someone since they were a child and people do change; it wouldn't be easy to simply stop being friends. Only Yahweh has the power to open our eyes (heart), see Case Law § **Psalms 34:15** KJV - "The eyes of the LORD Yahweh are upon the righteous, and his ears are open unto their cry. An enemy is someone who wants to see you suffer in any shape or form. Common sense lets us know when something harmful or deadly is imminent. When we see danger, naturally we should stay far away right? Nope, not when it is someone we consider a friend. According to Strong's Hebrew Concordance No. 340, enemy in Hebrew is Ayab (איב); verb: A primitive root; to hate (as one of an opposite tribe or party); hence to be hostile -- be an enemy.

See Case Law **§ Proverbs 16:30** KJV - "He shutteth his eyes to devise froward things: moving his lips he bringeth evil to pass." In ancient times, referring to Eastern civilization, hostility was a common aspect of intertribal and international dealings. Hostility could arise from land disputes, spiritual differences, or breaches of contractual agreements. The notion of bitterness also extends to the spiritual realm, where the people of Yahweh are often depicted as being at war with forces combative to Yahweh's will and purposes. Anytime someone gives you advice that turns out to be injurious, consider them an enemy. I have had people give me bad advice in family matters, business, work, and so on. The thing is, they knew exactly what they were doing but I never thought for a second that someone who calls you a friend would intentionally set you up for failure. See Case Law **§ Job 17:5** KJV - "He that speaketh flattery to his friends, even the eyes of his children shall fail." Me personally, if I do not care for someone I actually leave them alone. Therefore, I will not be calling or texting you. I will not bother you period. No, the enemy does the exact opposite. They will call, text and even come to your house as much as possible. These people know downright that they have ill will towards you. See Case Law **§ Job 16:9** KJV - "He teareth me in his wrath, who hateth me: he gnasheth upon me with his teeth; mine enemy sharpeneth his eyes upon me."

An enemy can be upfront with us more than we think, this is because they are marked by malevolence : having or showing unfriendly feelings. There have been many instances when a so-called friend picked up their phone to call me, only to start an argument with me. Now, I am very cautious when my phone rings. I think about what the conversation could possibly be about, et cetera. It's exhausting and frustrating when people waste your time. Some family members can be your enemy. Ever gone to a family member's house only to receive inhospitality from them? Ever had a friend that never invited you to their home? You ask yourself, "I have known this person for years and they visit my home all the time. What's the problem?". A healthy friendship is a give and take type of thing. An enemy will intentionally suck you dry however they can, emotionally, spiritually, financially, psychologically and mentally. See Case Law **§ 1 Samuel 18:29** KJV - "And Saul was yet the more afraid of David; and Saul became David's enemy continually." I believe Yahweh blesses each and every one of us with many gifts which in turn come through as talent; pure raw talent. It is up to each of us what we decide to do with this talent(s). When you are living your purpose or trying to, people closest to you do not always accept this well. To grow up with a childhood friend, or even a sibling and for them to see your success is like looking in a mirror.

See Case Law **§ 2 Chronicles 25:8** KJV - "But if thou wilt go, do it, be strong for the battle: Yahweh shall make thee fall before the enemy: for Yahweh hath power to help, and to cast down." I don't know anyone that wants to work in a hostile workplace. People with strong personalities can come off as intimidating to others. Someone who is mean to you at times could be intimidated by you; so they resort to retaliation of some sort. I don't know anyone that ever wants to be in a hostile environment alone. Acting against or in a contrary direction is a telltale sign of an enemy. For example, have you ever hosted an event and needed that so-called friend to be there and at the last minute they cancel? What about that time where you wanted to raise money for a business venture and no one helped or put a $1 towards it? I have plenty of experiences to share! See Case Law **§ Psalms 55:3** KJV - "Because of the voice of the enemy, because of the oppression of the wicked: for they cast iniquity upon me, and in wrath they hate me." The close watcher is always opposed to anything good you have going for yourself. What makes them happy is anything that is the opposite of what makes you happy. Anything unfavorable for you, is favorable in their eyes. These types of people lack the positive qualities that you may possess.

Another telltale sign of a close watcher is when they make sure you're juggling with more expenses than income: constituting a loss. Meaning, they are helping you make bad financial decisions. The close watcher is a so-called friend who will also deny the truth, reality, or validity of their behavior. Close watcher friends are individuals who lack self-esteem, dignity, self-respect and integrity. They see you moving forward in life head- strong. Though all you see are obstacles and bumps in the road. They apparently fail to acknowledge the struggles that led you to be where you are currently. They say misery loves company and sadly this is true for some. You have people out here debt free with the intention to stay that way. Here comes the close watch friend, encouraging you to spend money you don't have and pile up debt just like them. I experienced it myself, "girl, you can find a way to make that payment", "girl, you work hard; go ahead just do it". I have witnessed situations where so-called friends whose income was double of mine were actually broke but for the sake of public ridicule, they appeared to be well-off financially. You should never put someone in a financial bind especially when you do not know their overall financial status. Yes, the person on the other end should know better than to allow someone to put their back against the wall.

At the end of the day, it is unethical to intentionally set someone up to fail. Yahweh will deal with you one way or another. See Case Law § **Psalms 106:10** KJV - "And he saved them from the hand of him that hated them, and redeemed them from the hand of the enemy." The close watcher friend causes harm to you intentionally and unintentionally. How, you might ask? Well, for starters they were never your friend to begin with. For someone to unintentionally harm you is by default because they are unconscious for your wellbeing. Truth often comes through jokes. The close watcher friend has from time to time shown you dislike or opposition and you may choose to ignore it. I cannot tell you how many times indirect insults were thrown my way, whether over the phone or directly to my face. As time passed on, I had time to sit and reflect on what was said. It is not my loss; the friendship that is, but theirs. Jealousy and envy play a role with these types of people who simply refuse to just walk away and leave you alone. See Case Law § **Jeremiah 31:16** KJV - "Thus saith the LORD Yahweh; Refrain thy voice from weeping, and thine eyes from tears: for thy work shall be rewarded, saith the LORD Yahweh; and they shall come again from the land of the enemy."

The close watcher friend is as follows: opponent, foe, rival, enemy, adversary, competitor, attacker, archenemy and critic. They come initially as a so-called friend because they know you would not associate with them had they come straight up as your enemy. Just like Satan came into the garden with Adam and Eve, so come these close watchers. They are the biggest deceivers, not to you and I, but to themselves. The reason I mentioned jealousy plays a role is because the close watch friends are the ones who strive for the same things as you do. Here you are being your authentic self and they, lacking from within, must copy your every move. Instead of complementing you for your tenacity, here comes unnecessary criticism. A real friendship does not involve competition with one another but support and encouragement for each other. A real friend is one who wishes well to others: an admiring advocate or fan. The close watch so-called friend is the total opposite of someone who wants another person to be happy, prosperous, etc. Anyone can slip up and say things they shouldn't. Poisonous friends might seem to love circulating secrets around, even when you ask them to keep private information secret. Someone who continually breaks your trust likely doesn't care much about your feelings or you in general.

See Case Law § **Micah 7:8** KJV - "Rejoice not against me, O mine enemy: when I fall, I shall arise; when I sit in darkness, the LORD Yahweh shall be a light unto me." The close watcher friend regularly degrades you and makes you feel depressed, whether they use more subtle nasty tactics or outright insults. This is not a healthy relationship. The crazy part is, when you catch their slick remarks, they try to play it off. The close watcher friend will apologize real quick with no sincerity. These unapologetic attitudes suggest someone doesn't really care how their actions impact you. Spending time with a close friend ought to make you feel good, typically speaking. I know when I was hanging out with a close watcher friend, I couldn't wait for us to split ways. You are excited to meet up at first but as time goes on, comes the party pooper tactics begin. I remember going out to eat with my daughter and this so-called close watcher friend would always find a way to sneak her way in with us. I was always paying for our meals, it was as if I had 2 children to look after. There is nothing wrong with treating your friend out to eat. But when it becomes a habit of you always paying, something ain't right. See Case Law § **Deuteronomy 23:19** KJV - "Thou shalt not lend upon usury to thy brother; usury of money, usury of victuals, usury of any thing that is lent upon usury:"

It is against The Laws of יהוה to misuse or abuse your Hebrew family but this individual is not considered my family. See Case Law § **Deuteronomy 23:20** KJV - "Unto a stranger thou mayest lend upon usury; but unto thy brother thou shalt not lend upon usury: that the LORD Yahweh thy God may bless thee in all that thou settest thine hand to in the land whither thou goest to possess it." Long story short, I eventually stopped inviting this individual out with us, my daughter was like emah (mum) please do not bring such and such with us any more. The close watcher friend has a bad habit of comparing you to their other friends. For example, they like to point out tendencies you don't measure up to their other friends. I always responded, "okay, good for them"! The close watcher friend is your biggest hater. People have their own personal qualities and variations, and a solid friend will appreciate this. A real friend won't compare you to others or hint you're half less than another individual. The close watcher friend definitely uses peer pressure to get you to do things you'd prefer not to do. That so-called close watcher friend would easily entice you to open numerous credit cards (run your credit score too often which will hurt you in the long run). This close watcher friend does not care what you have going on.

They intentionally want to inflict harm on or towards you. See Case Law §

**Proverbs 28:8** KJV - "He that by usury and unjust gain increaseth his substance,

he shall gather it for him that will pity the poor." I remember intentionally avoiding

certain so-called friends because I knew they were up to no good. Yahweh 28

moral behavioral attributes do not exist in some people at all. They are incapable of

exuding these characteristics. The close watcher friends tend to drop in when

things are running good or when they want something, but when *you're* struggling,

you can't reach them at all. I remember one late night, a so-called close watcher

friend called me for five dollars, and my gut told me this was a test to see if I

would be a good friend to her in her time of need. Yahweh knows this was no test

but a setup for future bad borrowing habits that eventually led up to thousands of

dollars. I cut them off from any access to my money real quick and fast. How can

anyone take from a mother with a small child and be okay with themselves? See

Case Law § **Exodus 22:25** KJV - "If thou lend money to any of my people that is

poor by thee, thou shalt not be to him as an usurer, neither shalt thou lay upon him

usury." Let me be clear, this individual was not poor to me, at least that was what I

thought.

This individual may have been poor spiritually but not financially (I now know they are spiritually broke). This so-called close watcher friend made double the amount of money than me and that never stopped them from financially abusing me. All good things come to an end for people of that stature. Yahweh blesses those who are charitable and not just in means of money. See Case Law §

**Deuteronomy 15:6** KJV - "For the LORD Yahweh thy God blesseth thee, as he promised thee: and thou shalt lend unto many nations, but thou shalt not borrow; and thou shalt reign over many nations, but they shall not reign over thee."

The close watcher friend is all for manipulation. Anyone who tries to change things about you may rarely be a good friend. The close watcher friend will inevitably increase your stress levels. Even when they aren't with you, you might waste a lot of time reflecting back on their hostile interactions, which can make you feel troubled, grumpy, even absolutely awful. Let go and let Yahweh in your life. According to Strong's Hebrew Concordance No. 5782, watch in Hebrew is Awr (עוּר); verb: a primitive root (rather identical with awr through the idea of opening the eyes); to wake (literally or figuratively) -- (a-)wake(-n, up), lift up (self), X master, raise (up), stir up (self).

Generally speaking, everyone should be straightforward, open and honest when dealing with one another. Unfortunately, this is not always the case in our everyday lives. In ancient Hebrew civilization, the idea of awakening was not only physical but also spiritual and emotional. Hebrew Israelites often used the term in their verse and songs to describe Yahweh's interference in life events, calling on Him to wake and act on their behalf. The thought of awakening also carried implications of preparations and caution, superior qualities for a people often encountering physical and spiritual fights. See Case Law **§ Genesis 49:9** KJV - "Judah is a lion's whelp: from the prey, my son, thou art gone up: he stooped down, he couched as a lion, and as an old lion; who shall rouse him up?" The close watcher friend even makes you second guess yourself. Once you begin to question yourself, you might see yourself as a horrible friend. Even if you don't begin questioning yourself, you might find it challenging to trust others. See Case Law **§ Psalms 56:11** KJV - "In Yahweh have I put my trust: I will not be afraid what man can do unto me." The close watcher friend is someone with destructive behavior. Nothing good comes out of them nor from them. The close watcher friend has a goal in mind, and it is to watch your every move, make sure you do not advance in life, and make sure your life is much harder than it needs to be.

The close watcher friend is someone out to damage you irreparably. Their actions are meant to cause you to become bankrupt, impoverished, and ruined. How many times did you explain to your so-called close watcher friend that you could not attend an event, or you could not make that purchase and they find a way to persuade you to do otherwise? They are capable of subjecting you to frustration, failure, or disaster. I have witnessed some so-called close watcher friends cause physical, moral, economic, or social crashes to others. The people that I love, that are near and dear to my heart; I warn them when I see people with these tendencies. Unfortunately, some listen too late. See Case Law § **Proverbs 30:5** KJV - "Every word of Yahweh is pure: he is a shield unto them that put their trust in him." Any time someone brings disorder into your life, you better take action. The close watcher friend brings nothing but chaos and confusion. Ever felt helpless? Ever gotten yourself into a situation because of bad advice or you just could not come up with a solution to your problems? I bet that close watcher friend was of no help or use. It's overwhelming just thinking about it. A close watcher is an individual who prides themself on depriving you of joy, peace, love, support, friendship and more.

With such bad habits, they can cause you to be renounced or turned away from entirely; forsaken. For someone to cause you to appear mean, miserable, or contemptible is an unfortunate situation to be in. No one wants to deal with a wretched individual. See Case Law § **Psalms 71:1** KJV - "In thee, O LORD Yahweh, do I put my trust: let me never be put to confusion." If you waste a lot of time wishing a friend will treat you better, why not take a break from them for a while and see what changes? I personally have done this and believe it or not, it does make a difference. Some, on the other hand, I have made the decision to permanently leave them alone. See Case Law § **Nahum 1:7** KJV - "The LORD Yahweh is good, a strong hold in the day of trouble; and he knoweth them that trust in him." The close watcher friend needs boundaries set. Of course, this is normally done in the beginning of friendships, but from time to time they have to be revisited. Establish that you will not accept certain behaviors, such as hollering, dishonesty, spilling the beans, or slipping out on plans with no explanation. Time away from the friendship can aid you in analyzing your emotions and conjuring a clearer idea of what your next move should be. You will also notice how your life looks without that person in it.

For me, it was much more peaceful. I could actually hear my thoughts again. While the level of detail you deliver may rely on the incidents or your accounts with that person, never leave the close watcher friend with any uncertainty about the state of your friendship. Why would they want to end the friendship? It's been very beneficial to them using you as a pawn. They may cut you off or try twisting the story around to make you feel guilty. See Case Law **§ Zechariah 8:16** KJV - "These are the things that ye shall do; Speak ye every man the truth to his neighbour; execute the judgment of truth and peace in your gates:" If you decide to cut off communications or overall association with them, trust your gut and avoid reaching out or replying to their attempts to contact you. In time, you might consider the good times you shared and wonder if they've changed.

Think of why you ended the friendship. Revisiting your reasons could make you just as miserable again, so it's better to let some time lapse before you consider letting them back into your life. I left a so-called friend alone for 3 years and afterwards they treated me better. Before you consider allowing this individual to re-enter your life consider that it is common for them to encroach on your privacy. I knew an individual who just so happened to show up every time me and my daughter were getting ready for supper.

Every single time we were getting ready to leave to head out to run errands, it was as if they were using super powers to see what we had going on. They would make inquiries centered around what we had planned and where we were going. Then, me being naive, I would confess my plans to them only to have my quality time with my child infringed upon. This individual made it their business to "catch a ride" with me everywhere I went. They would be like, "oh, hey! I need to run to that store too"! It got so bad that at one point I just stopped answering my phone, closed my blinds to make it appear no one was home, or I made sure to go out of town so that way they couldn't include themselves in my plans. It was absolutely horrible, and this individual is older than me so you would think they would know better. It is better to let those close watching friends go on with their lives without you in it. Remember, they were not your friend to begin with so you are not losing anything. See Case Law **§ Psalms 85:11** KJV - "Truth shall spring out of the earth; and righteousness shall look down from heaven." You can discuss with someone how their behavior impacts you, but you can't make them change. They have to do this on their own, and not everyone is willing to do the work. They might promise to change and treat you better in the short-term.

But if they start insulting you again or if they are regressing into other patterns of poisonous behavior, you're better off moving on. See Case Law § **Proverbs 3:5 KJV** - "Trust in the LORD Yahweh with all thine heart; and lean not unto thine own understanding". The close watcher friend is a faultfinder. You will never do things good enough for them. Petty, nagging, or unreasonable criticism is all they have to offer you. They have a tendency to judge you harshly with no remorse. The close watcher gets pleasure from asking complicated questions that are meant to confuse, entrap, or entangle you in an argument. Count your blessings if you no longer tolerate them, "the close watcher so-called friend" that is. The close watcher friends are the main ones carping about every little thing the minute you link up with them. Leave them right where you found them.

# Chapter 4

The giving friend is a direct blessing from the giver, Yahweh. Do not abuse the friend that gives or else you can count your days to the end of something amazing. According to Strong's Hebrew Concordance No. 5414, give in Hebrew is Nathan (naw-than) (נתן); verb: a primitive root; to give, used with greatest latitude of application (put, make, etc.) -- add, apply, appoint, ascribe, assign, X avenge, X be ((healed)), bestow, bring (forth, hither), cast, cause, charge, come, commit, consider, count, + cry, deliver (up), direct, distribute, do, X doubtless, X without fail, fasten, frame, X get, give (forth, over, up), grant, hang (up), X have, X indeed, lay (unto charge, up), (give) leave, lend, let (out), + lie, lift up, make, + O that, occupy, offer, ordain, pay, perform, place, pour, print, X pull, put (forth), recompense, render, requite, restore, send (out), set (forth), shew, shoot forth (up), + sing, + slander, strike, (sub-)mit, suffer, X surely, X take, thrust, trade, turn, utter, + weep, + willingly, + withdraw, + would (to) God, yield.

In ancient Hebrew knowledge, the act of giving was deeply fixed in social and spiritual practices. Gifts and donations were essential to adoration and contractual agreements. The idea of being charitable was not only about material things but also about performing duties, promises, and proving favor. The act of being charitable was seen as a judgement of one's character and relationship with Yahweh and others. See Case Law **§ 2 Corinthians 9:7** KJV - "Every man according as he purposeth in his heart, so let him give; not grudgingly, or of necessity: for Yahweh loveth a cheerful giver." I love giving. When I give to another individual, I make it my business to go all out. There is something satisfying in giving to another soul, whether through gifts, information or some other kind of form. Yahweh is the biggest giver there is to exist. His creations include: you, me, the air we breathe, the food we eat, the clothes we wear, the water we drink and so forth. If I could earn a living from making personalized gifts, I wouldn't hesitate to. My daughter always tells me that I do too much! But it's just because of the joy it brings me. Just thinking about the other person on the other end receiving the gift and their facial expression brings me such joy.

Sometimes I feel the only reason people invite me to their events or any other type of gathering is because of my giving capacity. See Case Law **§ Genesis 28:22** KJV - "And this stone, which I have set for a pillar, shall be Yahweh's house: and of all that thou shalt give me I will surely give the tenth unto thee." Do not get me wrong, I am not complaining about giving to others. It's just that I am sincere in things that I do for others. My thoughtfulness is not always reciprocated or appreciated on the receiver's end. I think it's a wonderful gift to instill someone with confidence, encouragement and thoughtful gestures. Yahweh gave each and every one of us many gifts. When you put something into the possession of another for his or her use, you just performed the notion of giving. See Case Law **§ 1 Chronicles 22:12** KJV - "Only the LORD Yahweh give thee wisdom and understanding, and give thee charge concerning Israel, that thou mayest keep the law of the LORD Yahweh thy God." Another way we give is when we commit to one another as a trust or responsibility and usually for an expressed reason. The giver friend executes and delivers what they intend to. Who better to look out for you than a good friend? Yahweh is the best friend you will ever have and no one can compare to Him. Now with us being spiritual beings, we tend to make earthly so-called friends.

Yahweh can use anyone to get a message to you if He needs to. But when Yahweh allows a good-natured friend to enter your life, consider yourself blessed. I forget the saying, if you ever get a good friend in your lifetime. The point is a real good friend is a giver. They are always thinking of you and how they can contribute to you. I could be going through stressful times and yet I have found myself thinking about people that are near and dearest to me. Here I am in need and could use some help myself, but no! Instead of me taking care of myself, I often put my concerns on the backburner to help others in need. The giver friend is thoughtful and considerate. See Case Law **§ Psalms 28:4** KJV - "Give them according to their deeds, and according to the wickedness of their endeavours: give them after the work of their hands; render to them their desert." Your well- being is everything to someone who is sincere about you. A friend that gives will not take from you or put you in a position where it could cost you your livelihood. There is something satisfying about doing good to others. It's the right thing to do. Yahweh is a just God. See Case Law **§ Proverbs 11:1** KJV - "A false balance is abomination to the LORD Yahweh: but a just weight is his delight." In other words, do not deal falsely with others. Consumers are often cheated of their money based on this logic alone, not everyone reveres Yahweh as they should.

An abomination to Yahweh is anything regarded with disgust or hatred. For example, see Case Law **§ Proverbs 29:27** KJV - "An unjust man is an abomination to the just: and he that is upright in the way is abomination to the wicked." See Case Law **§ Proverbs 6:16 - 19** KJV - "These six things doth the LORD Yahweh hate: yea, seven are an abomination unto him: 17. A proud look, a lying tongue, and hands that shed innocent blood, 18. An heart that deviseth wicked imaginations, feet that be swift in running to mischief, 19. A false witness that speaketh lies, and he that soweth discord among brethren." A friend that gives, will take the time to consider your feelings. Ever go out of your way to please a friend? That, in some shape or form is a way of giving. Giving does not always have to be tangible. When you hear the word give, people tend to think of something they can see, touch, or taste. What about the feeling or connection we make when we give? Yahweh gave us life, this is something we can obviously see and feel right? See Case Law **§ Ecclesiastes 2:26** KJV - "For Yahweh giveth to a man that is good in his sight wisdom, and knowledge, and joy: but to the sinner he giveth travail, to gather and to heap up, that he may give to him that is good before Yahweh. This also is vanity and vexation of spirit."

When we pick up the phone to call someone, we are giving them our time. Thus, your time is valuable. Yahweh is a God of action and will not waste your time. A giver friend will always be respectful of your time. They are punctual people you can depend on. Boundaries are important in relationships. A giver definitely has their hand open (literally) to those they care about. According to Strong's Hebrew Concordance No. 3027, an open hand in Hebrew means Yawd (יד'), noun feminine: a primitive word; a hand (the open one (indicating power, means, direction, etc.), in distinction from kaph, the closed one); used (as noun, adverb, etc.) In a great variety of applications, both literally and figuratively, both proximate and remote (as follows) -- (+ be) able, X about, + armholes, at, axletree, because of, beside, border, X bounty, + broad, (broken-)handed, X by, charge, coast, + consecrate, + creditor, custody, debt, dominion, X enough, + fellowship, force, X from, hand(-staves, -y work), X he, himself, X in, labour, + large, ledge, (left-)handed, means, X mine, ministry, near, X of, X order, ordinance, X our, parts, pain, power, X presumptuously, service, side, sore, state, stay, draw with strength, stroke, + swear, terror, X thee, X by them, X themselves, X thine own, X thou, through, X throwing, + thumb, times, X to, X under, X us, X wait on, (way-)side, where, + wide, X with (him, me, you), work, + yield, X yourselves.

See Case Law § **Deuteronomy 15:11** KJV - "For the poor shall never cease out of the land: therefore I command thee, saying, Thou shalt open thine hand wide unto thy brother, to thy poor, and to thy needy, in thy land." Yahweh commands us to be generous, charitable, and merciful. A giver friend has these characteristics, so naturally they will help when they are able. In old Eastern society, the hand was a symbol of strength, power, and authority. The open hand was often connected with the skill to act, produce, or ruin. The hand was also a symbol of blessing and mercy, as seen in the custom of placing hands on someone to give a blessing or influence. In the biblical setting, Yahweh's hand is repeatedly referenced as a symbol of His power and interference in life matters. It's always better to give than to receive. Afterall, look how much we receive from Yahweh: knowledge, wisdom, understanding, life, love, financial security, shelter, and necessities to sustain our lives. He is constantly giving to us so why can't we return the favor to others. See Case Law § **Isaiah 62:3** KJV - "Thou shalt also be a crown of glory in the hand of the LORD Yahweh, and a royal diadem in the hand of thy God Yahweh." A giver friend will go out of their way to make sure you are happy. To experience someone treating you as if you are the best person walking the Earth is pretty special. Entertainment is a no- sweat matter for a giver friend, they will go all out.

A giver friend is a real good friend. They are genuinely interested in your aspirations and genuinely happy for your success. Their faces light up when you share good news. They inspire you to grow in life. Motivation is one of the best traits in a giver friend. See Case Law **§ Psalms 139:10** KJV - "Even there shall thy hand lead me, and thy right hand shall hold me." To be able to give is a wonderful blessing. Though Yahweh is the most important giver we could ever receive, we still must also be givers ourselves. See Case Law **§ Psalms 63:4** KJV - "Thus will I bless thee while I live: I will lift up my hands in thy name." We must understand that there are so many qualities that constitute a giver friend, and understanding this, and what you want from a friendship is the first key to recognizing the *healthy* traits in a good friend. Communication is key. Having a good friend *doesn't* always mean they will respond to each text within moments, but they should respond at some point. Life is about giving and receiving. See Case Law **§ Psalms 145:10** KJV - "All thy works shall praise thee, O LORD Yahweh; and thy saints shall bless thee." A friend that's a giver will not continually mock you. They will bother to respond to you and send a message about how much they value you. People who are givers tend to be considerate of others. I'd say they are selfless individuals.

I have friends that live a long distance from me. I do not get to talk to them often but when we do reconnect, we spend hours on the phone like it was yesterday. Friendships grow and change as we get mature, but a friend that's a giver, is a life long friend indeed. I believe friendships that serve our wants and needs are the premises for deep-rooted relationships. A friend that is a giver is always thinking about others, they tend to be pure at heart and selfless individuals. We all should strive to be like an open hand; that is one continuously giving to others. It starts with charitable acts. See Case Law § **Deuteronomy 10:18** KJV - "He doth execute the judgment of the fatherless and widow, and loveth the stranger, in giving him food and raiment." When we lend a helping hand, we are participating in benevolence. According to Strong's Hebrew Concordance No. 2616, kindness in Hebrew is Chacad (chaw-sad (חסד); verb: a primitive root; properly, perhaps to bow (the neck only (compare chanan) in courtesy to an equal), i.e. To be kind; also (by euphem. (compare barak), but rarely) to reprove -- shew self merciful, put to shame. In ancient Hebrew Israelite civilization, the notion of chacad was vital to preserving friendly and domestic bonds. It was anticipated that people would act with kindness and loyalty within their society and family, mirroring the contractual agreement between Yahweh and His people.

This principle of contractual commitment was key to Hebrew Israelites' understanding of their union with Yahweh, who is often characterized as acting with chasad regarding His people. See Case Law **§ Isaiah 11:4** KJV - "But with righteousness shall he judge the poor, and reprove with equity for the meek of the earth: and he shall smite the earth with the rod of his mouth, and with the breath of his lips shall he slay the wicked." We learn from Strong's Hebrew Concordance No. 2603, to have grace and mercy in Hebrew is Chanan (Chaw-nan (חָנַן), verb: a primitive root (compare chanah); properly, to bend or stoop in kindness to an inferior; to favor, bestow; causatively to implore (i.e. Move to favor by petition) -- beseech, X fair, (be, find, shew) favour(-able), be (deal, give, grant (gracious(-ly), intreat, (be) merciful, have (shew) mercy (on, upon), have pity upon, pray, make supplication, X very. See Case Law **§ Jeremiah 2:19** KJV - "Thine own wickedness shall correct thee, and thy backslidings shall reprove thee: know therefore and see that it is an evil thing and bitter, that thou hast forsaken the LORD Yahweh thy God, and that my fear is not in thee, saith the Lord Yahweh of hosts."

In ancient Hebrew Israelite knowledge, blessings and favor were highly treasured traits, both in mortal relationships and in one's union with Yahweh. The thought of Chanan mirrors the contractual agreement between Yahweh and the Children of Israel, where Yahweh, as a sovereign and loving Creator, gives His blessing to His chosen people. This favor is not garnered, but a present, stressing the unjustified blessings that Yahweh provides the world. The notion of Yahweh's mercy was pivotal to Hebrew Israelites' realization of their identity and their relationship with Yahweh. The friend who is a giver, is a gift from Yahweh. See Case Law **§ Proverbs 17:8** KJV - "A gift is as a precious stone in the eyes of him that hath it: whithersoever it turneth, it prospereth." To be able to bless one another is a gift. According to Strong's Hebrew Concordance No. 1288, to bless, to kneel in Hebrew is Barak (baw-rahk (ברך); verb: a primitive root; to kneel; by implication to bless God (as an act of adoration), and (vice-versa) man (as a benefit); also (by euphemism) to curse (God or the king, as treason) -- X abundantly, X altogether, X at all, blaspheme, bless, congratulate, curse, X greatly, X indeed, kneel (down), praise, salute, X still, thank. Remember to always be thankful. For the greatest giver is Yahweh.

There is beauty in being a giver. There is favor in being a giver. There are blessings in being a giver. Blessed is everyone who blesses. See Case Law § **Genesis 12:3** KJV - "And I will bless them that bless thee, and curse him that curseth thee: and in thee shall all families of the earth be blessed." The Hebrew verb barak originally means to bless. It is applied in various spaces to signify the act of blessing, which can be interpreted as creating heavenly favor, voicing gratitude, or presenting prosperity. The word also suggests the act of kneeling, which is often connected with worship or displaying reverence. In the scriptures, barak is used to depict Yahweh's blessing upon individuals, the blessings society gives upon one another, and the blessings given to Yahweh in worship. See Case Law § **Genesis 26:4** KJV - "And I will make thy seed to multiply as the stars of heaven, and will give unto thy seed all these countries; and in thy seed shall all the nations of the earth be blessed;" In ancient Hebrew Israelite society, blessings were counted as powerful and meaningful. They were often proclaimed by patriarchs, priests, and kings, and were thought to have noticeable effects on the souls of those who accepted them. Blessings were essential to contractual agreements, domestic bonds, and collective praise. The act of kneeling, related with barak, was a physical demeanor of obedience, humbleness, and respect, often carried out during prayer or worship.

It is a privilege to be in alignment with the Giver, for Yahweh shall always preserve the righteous. Respecting boundaries is very important. A friend that's a giver will automatically do this. According to Strong's Hebrew Concordance No. 8159, respect in Hebrew is Sha'ah (שׁעה); verb: a primitive root; to gaze at or about (properly, for help); by implication, to inspect, consider, compassionate, be nonplussed (as looking around in amazement) or bewildered -- depart, be dim, be dismayed, look (away), regard, have respect, spare, turn. A giver is always respectful of others' time regardless of anything. I am sure you have witnessed in your lifetime someone wasting another individuals' time. It's very rude to do that to someone especially when you already had in mind how you'd like things to conclude. See Case Law § **Proverbs 28:21** KJV - "To have respect of persons is not good: for for a piece of bread that man will transgress." Yahweh teaches us to be wise. When someone shows you high or special praise for something, be grateful. Not many people are considerate. That is what makes a giver friend stand out. In ancient Hebrew civilization, the act of looking or staring, gave profound clues of appreciation, opinion, or thought. The idea of Yahweh looking upon someone or something was important, as it suggested divine awareness, approval, or condemnation.

Thus, it mirrors the lineage stance of the Hebrew Israelites' consciousness of Yahweh, who is diligently involved with His people. The Hebrew verb sha'ah firstly means to look or stare, often with the indication of paying attention or perceiving something with well-being or favor. It can indicate a sense of turning one's heart or thought towards a matter or someone. In the place of the Bible, it is often used to depict Yahweh's observance or regard towards people or devotions. See Case Law **§ Deuteronomy 1:17** KJV - "Ye shall not respect persons in judgment; but ye shall hear the small as well as the great; ye shall not be afraid of the face of man; for the judgment is Yahweh's: and the cause that is too hard for you, bring it unto me, and I will hear it." A giver friend is a supportive friend who displays genuine happiness when you achieve your goals, dreams, and aspirations. Ever tell a so-called friend some good news, like you just got that promotion you've been working on and to your surprise it means absolutely nothing to them? Altruism is a remarkable characteristic. A giver is always concerned about the welfare of others. We know for a fact that Yahweh is a true giver. He is always concerned about His people. The righteous people of the Earth belong to Yahweh, and they are givers!

When Yahweh considers someone worthy of high regard like King Dawid, you are worthy and of high value to Him. What a wonderful feeling to know Yahweh thinks so highly of you and actually has respect for you. That is something to give thanks for. A giving friend not only has respect for their friend, they also appreciate them. When we value or admire the very thing placed before us, we grow to have an appreciation for it. See Case Law **§ Exodus 2:25** KJV - "And Yahweh looked upon the children of Israel, and Yahweh had respect unto them." A giver friend will recognize you with gratitude. When something is appreciated, it increases the value of it. I have personally witnessed a giver friend compromising for the sake of preserving a relationship. Giving is not always easy for some people. There is a hefty risk in both trust and susceptibility. This is the bedrock for being a good friend. It is wise to treasure a friend that is a giver, for they are something of great worth and value. A collection of precious things. See Case Law **§ Psalms 138:6** KJV - "Though the LORD Yahweh be high, yet hath he respect unto the lowly: but the proud he knoweth afar off."

A giver friend will consider or rate you highly because they actually value you. You will know your value when Yahweh finds favor in you and opens doors that no man can close. When Yahweh places good people in your life, it's good to rate or scale them in usefulness, importance, or general worth. Finding value in others is like going on a treasure hunt to seek out your counterparts. See Case Law **§ Proverbs 28:20** KJV - "A faithful man shall abound with blessings: but he that maketh haste to be rich shall not be innocent." I pray you can come to an agreement with me when I say there is an unwavering emotion that comes with being a giver. No one could ever be a better giver than Yahweh. He is in control of everything. We live our lives through His blessings and through His Will. We must acknowledge Yahweh in everything we do or He will not bless it, whatever that may be. See Case Law **§ Proverbs 3:6** KJV - "In all thy ways acknowledge him, and he shall direct thy paths." People will disappoint you but Yahweh will not. When you need a roof over your head, here comes Yahweh providing you with shelter. Back in the day, it was a standard to build your own home. Nowadays, you need a building permit or a contractors license to even do so, unless you take the owner-builder permit path.

See Case Law § **Jeremiah 29:5** KJV - "Build ye houses, and dwell in them; and plant gardens, and eat the fruit of them;" We are given new chances each and every day to make positive changes. For it is Yahweh that allows us to wake up and see another day. Once you come to the realization that Yahweh is in absolute control, if you're wise, you will start to think differently in your approach in your waking life. A real friend is with you throughout separation, sickness, and difficulties in life. Not just when it is handy for them. Someone who is a friend, knows you and welcomes who you are and your choices in life. They would not try to change you. Yahweh on the other hand, He does want us to be perfect and so yes, He would cause you to change if need be. See Case Law § **Matthew 5:48** KJV - "Be ye therefore perfect, even as your Father Yahweh which is in heaven is perfect." This should hit you differently. The main reason you will always feel at ease around a good friend is because you know they will not talk behind your back and because you know they're loyal. How many of us can say that? At the end of the day, Yahweh will be your best giving friend outside of spiritual beings. It is a fact that you cannot place a value on a friend that is a giver, especially Yahweh. They are worth more than money can buy.

# Chapter 5

Let us discuss what a taker is. A taker is someone who does exactly that and nothing more. According to Strong's Hebrew Concordance No. 3947, the word take in Hebrew is Laqach (law-kakh') (לקח); verb: a primitive root; to take (in the widest variety of applications) -- accept, bring, buy, carry away, drawn, fetch, get, infold, X many, mingle, place, receive(-ing), reserve, seize, send for, take (away, -ing, up), use, win. How many times in your life have you come across a so-called friend that does nothing but take from you? Take your time, money, health etc. Takers are self-attentive and put their own concerns before others' needs. They push to gain as much as viable from their dealings while chipping in as little as they can in return. See Case Law **§ Ecclesiasticus 6:13** KJV - "Separate thyself from thine enemies, and take heed of thy friends." A taker friend is someone who mainly concentrates on their own needs and wants.

In ancient Hebrew Israelite society, the act of taking often detailed official agreements or contracts, especially in the place of marriage or property deals. The notion of taking a wife, for example, was not simply a personal decision but a mutual and legal act that affected families and from time to time entire tribes. Likewise, taking ownership of land or goods often required proper procedures and was deeply ingrained in the lively and legal blueprints of the time.

See Case Law § **Isaiah 59:7** KJV - "Their feet run to evil, and they make haste to shed innocent blood: their thoughts are thoughts of iniquity; wasting and destruction are in their paths." I knew a friend whose friend would always invite themselves over to this friend's house, eat their food, drink their liquor and let them foot the bill when or if they went out to eat! Yeah, I was like you need to tell them to go home and cook for themselves. This lady would even ask to use this lady's credit cards! Takers are the worst! Takers only reach out when they require something from you. The signs of a taker include: constantly asking for favors, rarely repaying, boastful about themselves, and not being supportive when you need them. It's not great and they're often dangerous. Think about it. A taker does not care about your well-being. I have come across a lot of takers in my lifetime.

See Case Law **§ Ecclesiasticus 11:33** KJV - "Take heed of a mischievous man, for he worketh wickedness; lest he bring upon thee a perpetual blot." A taker will only be a taker for so long. Every dog has its day. The first thing you've got to do is recognize when you're around takers. It is wise to identify them in advance so you can cut them off. Ever been in a situation where you just got an advancement and they need a job? All of a sudden you're best friends again! Your phone starts to ring from this particular individual. All of a sudden they want to go grab a bite to eat and so forth! Spare me the drama. See Case Law **§ Proverbs 1:19** KJV - "So are the ways of every one that is greedy of gain; which taketh away the life of the owners thereof." The scripture points out that Yahweh has the power to give and the take away at the same time. See Case Law **§ Job 1:21** KJV - "And said, Naked came I out of my mother's womb, and naked shall I return thither: the LORD Yahweh gave, and the LORD Yahweh hath taken away; blessed be the name of the LORD Yahweh." Thus, we should be grateful for what we have and where we are in life. Yahweh teaches us to give and receive in portions. It's never a good idea to be greedy. Do not worry about greedy people who constantly take advantage of you, for Yahweh has something in store for them.

Takers are interested in their wants, their dreams, and their needs. Not yours. See Case Law **§ Psalms 37:21** KJV - "The wicked borroweth, and payeth not again: but the righteous sheweth mercy, and giveth." You go out of your way to help them with a project at work. Check this out, you go out of your way to make life better for your friend. But when you want something, they have an excuse as to why they can't assist you. See Case Law **§ Proverbs 28:9** KJV - "He that turneth away his ear from hearing the law, even his prayer shall be abomination." I get personally annoyed when someone tells me they don't have time. Yes, you do. The taker enjoys as much time as anyone else. They're just applying their time on something else they believe to be more meaningful than you and your demands. See Case Law **§ 1 Maccabees 2:68** KJV - "Recompense fully the heathen, and take heed to the commandments of the law." Takers do this when others talk, takers fantasize, think concerning their reply, or just wait for a hesitation in the discussion so they can shift the subject to something they want to talk about. I had a friend tell me one time how she went out of her way to take a gift to one of her so-called friends who lived out of state. The friend called her to tell her she was on her way while it was daylight.

Fast forward, 5 hours later she arrived when it was pitch dark. No explanation, no apology; no nothing. The so-called friend took the gift and went about her way. She later shared with me how upset her husband was because he was so tired from the long drive they made just to bring the gift. Some people can be selfish. Takers do not take into consideration how you feel, your children or spouse if you have any. See Case Law **§ Proverbs 25:8** KJV - "Go not forth hastily to strive, lest thou know not what to do in the end thereof, when thy neighbour hath put thee to shame." A taker does not listen. Remember I said this. We share our hearts with a taker and they don't value you. You see a shone look over their eyes and likewise they start telling you about their troubles. A taker feels like you owe them something. Some examples of this include: "Where did you get that purse from? Can I borrow it? How did you find that job that's paying so much? Are they hiring? Girl, where did you get those shoes from, can I wear them? I am moving next week, could you help me cover the cost? I am hosting a product launch party, could I use your house to host it instead of my place? You went out to eat last night and did not invite me? Girl, what are you cooking? Where's my plate? Bro, let me hold $10 til next week. Remember I came to your event to show support?"

Just a heads-up: If you are a taker, you will not endure real love nor have a healthy union at home. And if you are a taker at work, you will not progress with a fruitful crew or loyal clients. See Case Law **§ Proverbs 19:2** KJV - "Also, that the soul be without knowledge, it is not good; and he that hasteth with his feet sinneth." A selfish individual will ask you for a ride and not offer to put gas in your car. We see so-called government officials taking bribes that will only benefit them. We have plenty of takers in so-called government roles doing exactly that. Do you see so-called leaders taking a pay cut to help reduce taxes? See Case Law **§ Proverbs 28:22** - KJV - "He that hasteth to be rich hath an evil eye, and considereth not that poverty shall come upon him." You know exactly what I'm talking about. Most of the time takers do not call their so-called friends until they need something. We are always the one making the phone call, just to see how they are doing. A taker always wants more even though they give little to nothing in return. All of this behavior is discouraging and unmotivating. It can cause you to want to give up on being a giver because it's like what's the point. We do become disheartened when someone keeps intentionally abusing you for whatever reason. Though Yahweh teaches us to be charitable, it can be challenging.

See Case Law **§ Jeremiah 22:13** KJV - "Woe unto him that buildeth his house by unrighteousness, and his chambers by wrong; that useth his neighbour's service without wages, and giveth him not for his work;" Life is about giving and taking. Some people are all like "gimme, gimme, gimme", and they take more than necessary. Takers are people who have a lot of issues and demands. You know who they are. They have a history that is typically chaotic and the relationship predominately coincides with you doing things for them. You give, they take. Do not expect the taker to be there for you or you will be upset. I had a male friend who is always showing up for his so-called friends' events, business ventures, etc. Wherever he had similar situations, they were a no show every single time. For years this man supported them and it was never reciprocated. See Case Law § **Ecclesiasticus 27:36** KJV - "Whoso diggeth a pit shall fall therein: and he that setteth a trap shall be taken therein." Takers satisfy our want to feel significant. A taker will satisfy your urge to help people and feel good about yourself. How many wealthy takers do you know? A taker has nothing to give. Think about it, they are always holding their hand out begging. Believe it or not, you exist in a takers life to aid them, not the other way around. Yahweh teaches us to practice benevolence.

See Case Law § **Psalms 119: 143** KJV - "Trouble and anguish have taken hold on me: yet thy commandments are my delights." You should know that a taker is not your friend. Do not deceive yourself unless you plan to self-destruct. I remember while attending public school, how takers would be "friendly" only to get what they wanted. As an adult, I am still dealing with this sadly. Takers feed your ego by convincing you how lost they would be without you. They want you there to help them steer the disturbing parts of their lives. A taker can turn to you when they need a job, or when they need a place to stay, or when they need a favor. The list goes on. But takers turn away when you come to them. You cannot be taken advantage of unless you allow it. Disconnect your charity from your brotherhood or sisterhood. You can help humanity by aiding those who are takers as long as your expectations of repayment are practical. See Case Law § **Hebrews 13:6** KJV - "So that we may boldly say, The Lord Yahweh is my helper, and I will not fear what man shall do unto me." When the friendship is real, control is balanced. It is a mixture of taking and giving. We were meant to live a life that is rich, especially when you allow more people in it. Adulthood does not mean we have to accept imperfections. It is Yahweh's law that we strive to be perfect. See Case Law § **Deuteronomy 18:13** KJV - "Thou shalt be perfect with the LORD Yahweh thy God."

Takers see other people as opportunities, they do not see them as individuals. As a reader of this book, I guarantee you that you have met a self-focused individual in your lifetime. A taker will always be slack or lacking. The minute you need something they disappear, the minute they need something it's the end of the world. I had an experience where this taker got mad at me because I left her behind to take care of personal business. I mean the nerve of people! I've had constant phone calls that I was not able to answer immediately. Still, they kept calling me. By the time I did answer the phone I knew an argument was coming! Thankfully, I was prepared and handled the situation like a pro. I told that taker where they could go with their foolishness. See Case Law § **Psalms 74:22** KJV - "Arise, O Yahweh, plead thine own cause: remember how the foolish man reproacheth thee daily." According to Strong's Hebrew Concordance No. 1214, selfish in Hebrew is Batsa (בצע), verb: a primitive root to break off, i.e. (usually) plunder; figuratively, to finish, or (intransitively) stop -- (be) covet(- ous), cut (off), finish, fulfill, gain (greedily), get, be given to (covetousness), greedy, perform, be wounded. In so-called relationships which include marriages, there seems to be many examples where one will give more willingly than the other.

See Case Law § **Romans 13:9** KJV - "For this, Thou shalt not commit adultery, Thou shalt not kill, Thou shalt not steal, Thou shalt not bear false witness, Thou shalt not covet; and if there be any other commandment, it is briefly comprehended in this saying, namely, Thou shalt love thy neighbour as thyself." In ancient Hebrew Israelite society, and countless ancient civilizations, wealth and personal property were always seen as signs of Yahweh's blessing. Nevertheless, the Hebrew Israelite Scriptures continually warn against the pursuing of wealth through unethical means. The prophets and wisdom- written works, in detail, stress justice, equity, and the dangers of greed. The word batsa mirrors a cultural and spiritual understanding that true prosperity is not achieved through manipulation or jealousy but through righteousness and following Yahweh's laws. See Case Law § **Exodus 18:21** KJV - "Moreover thou shalt provide out of all the people able men, such as fear Yahweh, men of truth, hating covetousness; and place such over them, to be rulers of thousands, and rulers of hundreds, rulers of fifties, and rulers of tens:" A taker's behavior can worsen over time due to them becoming dependent on the giver. I want to add that it is never a good idea to have someone always giving either.

A healthy relationship must have balance. See Case Law § **Leviticus 19:35** KJV - "Ye shall do no unrighteousness in judgment, in meteyard, in weight, or in measure." The Hebrew verb "batsa" at first carries the idea of cutting or breaking off, often in the place of gaining something through unjust or violent means. It is continually used to describe the act of gaining wealth or property through greed, envy, or deceptive practices. The term carries an unfavorable indication, pinpointing actions that are morally and ethically questionable, especially in the search of material gain. A giver is negatively impacted in an unbalanced partnership. I wonder if the taker feels exceptionally positive about themselves most of the time (sarcasm, of course). I am sure a giver would feel good because they are actually doing something that allows them to give back and then some. The taker is always looking for more. As in, what is the manner in which they can receive something else? There is little contentment. Oblivious to how much you give, it's not sufficient for them. See Case Law § **Proverbs 21:15** KJV - "It is joy to the just to do judgment: but destruction shall be to the workers of iniquity."

Repaying someone is seldom considered by a taker. See Case Law § **Psalms 37:21** KJV - "The wicked borroweth, and payeth not again: but the righteous sheweth mercy, and giveth." Could we say a so-called taker is wicked? People that are takers don't want to help someone else intentionally. One of the character traits of a taker is that they will not hearken unto what is being said. You can have a whole dialogue concerning this person waiting for their feedback, but they do not care. Sooner or later, there's a realization that the taker only has the giver around for selfish reasons. You will eventually get tired of their nonsense and want nothing to do with them. There's light at the end of the tunnel. You cannot change someone who only takes. A taker has to want to change for the better on their own. It is never a good idea to try and change someone. I learned the hard way in my personal life. I have learned to let people be and do the best I can to not allow what they do affect me. Long story short, keep moving forward with your life. According to Strong's Hebrew Concordance No. 2498, change in Hebrew is Chalaph (חלאפ); verb: a primitive root; properly, to slide by, i.e. (by implication) to hasten away, pass on, spring up, pierce or change -- abolish, alter, change, cut off, go on forward, grow up, be over, pass (away, on, through), renew, sprout, strike through.

Takers have a crooked fantasy of their dominance, convincing themselves to be contributors and thoughtful to their mates instead of the selfish, arrogant, and begging partners that they are. See Case Law **§ Jeremiah 13:23** KJV - "Can the Ethiopian change his skin, or the leopard his spots? then may ye also do good, that are accustomed to do evil." Some people seem to find a problem in their lives and actually do want to change their bad habits. Others don't appear to be capable of taking favorable steps like that. People who are takers seem to repeat patterns that are self-destructive because they are unable to hear or accept others' advice. I am sure you can relate to this. I have tried countless times to help someone change for the better. I have told them things they could do, but they would not listen. Careless individuals spend years living a certain way, and that way alters their truth and their worldview. Hard- headed people are difficult to begin with. The Hebrew verb chalaph originally carries the idea of passing or changing. It can relate to the physical act of passing by or through something, as well as the figurative sense of change or renewal. In various settings, it can suggest the shift from one state to another, such as the altering of garments, the rebirth of strength, or the path of time. Some people feel change is like walking along a cliff while blindfolded.

This causes people to deny the presence of change. Change is intended to bring something differentiable. It will not happen overnight and we must try and forge ahead. See Case Law **§ Psalms 15:4** KJV - "In whose eyes a vile person is contemned; but he honoureth them that fear the LORD Yahweh. He that sweareth to his own hurt, and changeth not." In ancient Hebrew Israelite society, the notion of change and renewal was big. It was often associated with Yahweh's ability to revise deals and people. The continuous nature of days and the renewal of life were seen as deliberations of divine order and Yahweh. The usage of chalaph in the Hebrew Bible often accentuates Yahweh's sovereignty in creating change and renewal, either in nature, personal matters, or spiritual life. Yahweh does not change. He is, after all, the Creator. See Case Law **§ Malachi 3:6** KJV - "For I am the LORD Yahweh, I change not; therefore ye sons of Jacob are not consumed." However, you and I are instructed to change especially if we have evil or wicked ways of acting and thinking. Change is an exodus from the past and a taker has to accept this one way or the other. A taker won't confess to you when out of line but will expect you to apologize to them. Adjustments are necessary when it comes to change. It is met with resistance when it makes people feel stupid.

Takers don't regret taking from you, but they regret not taking enough from you. Change is certainly more work for anyone. A taker will not want to change because it is already devastating to them in the first place. They need to have the last say in discourses. Sadly, many people are forced to change their whole outlook to account for new facts that challenge their beloved beliefs. Takers aren't inspired to know, care, or do anything unless it lands them something. See Case Law **§ 1 Corinthians 6:2** KJV - "Do ye not know that the saints shall judge the world? and if the world shall be judged by you, are ye unworthy to judge the smallest matters?" They hold everyone else liable but avoid holding themselves accountable. Have you noticed a taker talk much more than they listen? The list of bad attributes of a taker can be discouraging. Now, there is nothing wrong with receiving from others when they are genuine. I'd respect a taker who can be honest and upfront with me that they're here to collect and that's it. It's the ones who present themselves as sheep when they are actually wolves that you should steer clear of. Yahweh hates a liar. See Case Law **§ Proverbs 17:4** KJV - "A wicked doer giveth heed to false lips; and a liar giveth ear to a naughty tongue". In life we have the ability to make ourselves different in some particular way.

To alter oneself may be seen as cliche but in reality it's not. A taker has the ability to take a radically different approach in life but in a good way. When we transform ourselves in order to bring about change, it should be to benefit everyone. Takers could learn to replace their destitute ways with wealthy ones like charity. Change starts at home. You have to be willing to put yourself out there and take a chance. Learn to say no to takers. There is nothing wrong with helping someone who happens to be a taker. Just be sure to set limits as far as what you're willing to do. You are not anyone's automated teller machine unless you want to be. No one can force you to do anything you don't want to do. Set boundaries for yourself when dealing with a taker. See Case Law **§ Exodus 22:25** KJV - "If thou lend money to any of my people that is poor by thee, thou shalt not be to him as an usurer, neither shalt thou lay upon him usury." A taker has to want to switch their way of thinking and doing. Old bad habits should die and new good habits should be born. Some things never change like gravity. Bad habits should change. We should want to become different. A makeover might sound like a lot but it is necessary sometimes. One must understand that change is necessary in order to grow.

If we choose to remain stagnant in life, we will experience spiritual, mental, psychological and emotional hurdles. Let's be honest with ourselves, change leads to personal growth. Change is inevitable. This is a fact. Opportunities come from change, but we must be open to it. If you are a taker, just know that now is the time to make up your mind and change. Tomorrow is not promised; therefore, we should live everyday with high expectations. Yahweh commands that we live righteous lives. There are 28 moral behavioral attributes and they are: righteous, just, upright, honest, straightforward, open, honorable, good, well-behaved, excellent, right conduct, principle, ethical, truth, right, rule, teaching, conform, virtuous, chaste, action, mind, feeling, will, character, nature, judgment and caution. We must exude all of these qualities, and none are exempt. See Case Law **§ Habakkuk 1:4** KJV - "Therefore the law is slacked, and judgment doth never go forth: for the wicked doth compass about the righteous; therefore wrong judgment proceedeth." Taking from someone for the fun of it is wrong. We must end bad, mean, cruel, and wicked ideas that come across our minds. If a negative thought comes to mind, immediately change your mind to something positive.

If something negative happens to you, do not allow it to hold you back from great things in life. Take responsibility for your actions. It is always better to give than to receive. However, do not be fooled. Every change produces both positive and negative consequences. You have got to determine when enough is enough, should you decide to keep a taker in your life.

# Chapter 6

Your health matters. Yahweh is all for selfcare. See Case Law **§ 1 Timothy 3:5** KJV - "(For if a man know not how to rule his own house, how shall he take care of the assembly of Yahweh?)". Only a good friend would encourage you to take care of yourself. You should already know to take care of yourself. See Case Law **§ 1 Thessalonians 4:9** KJV - "But as touching brotherly love ye need not that I write unto you: for ye yourselves are taught of Yahweh to love one another." Having a healthy relationship is vital to your well-being. According to Strong's Hebrew Concordance, health in Hebrew is Arwkah (ארוכה); Noun Feminine: or rarukah {ar-oo-kaw'}; feminine passive participle of 'arak (in the sense of restoring to soundness); wholeness (literally or figuratively) -- health, made up, perfected. The condition of being sound in body, mind, or spirit is a good sign of perfect health.

There are times in life when we have to nurse ourselves back to health. It could be from a bad breakup, or over exhausting yourself for a job, or you had an unfortunate accident. The point is we all fall sick sometimes and need time to heal. The Hebrew word arwkah initially relates to the idea of healing or restoration, often in a physical or spiritual meaning. It gives the idea of something being made whole or rejuvenated to its original state. In the place of the Bible, it is constantly used to describe the healing of wounds or the restoration of health. See Case Law **§ Proverbs 16:24** KJV - "Pleasant words are as an honeycomb, sweet to the soul, and health to the bones." We tend to turn to other people for various reasons. Every single day, we have many interactions. There are undeniable health benefits from being in a healthy relationship. When we are immersed in a positive relationship, we live longer. Who wants to be around a person that drains them of their energy, power, and resources? Certainly not me! I am sure you have encountered individuals in your life that caused your good mood to dramatically shift. I cannot emphasize enough how blissful you'll feel to be free of negative people. Free from drama, arguments, headaches, pain, whether physical, psychological, mental and spiritual. If you listen to your instincts, they pretty much give you a warning when something does not feel right.

In ancient Hebrew Israelite civilization, health and healing were seen as blessings from Yahweh. Illness or injury often connoted consequences during those times. The thought of arwkah would have been perceived not only as physical healing, but also as a sign of divine favor and renewal. Hebrew Israelites know that Yahweh is the ultimate healer, and prayers for arwkah would have been normal in times of sickness or pain. When we reduce stress from our lives, it does a lot of good. Practicing healthy habits increases longevity. See Case Law **§ Psalms 67:2** KJV - "That thy way may be known upon earth, thy saving health among all nations." It is a known fact that lower levels of stress hormones like cortisol, allows one to heal quicker than normal. You can go all your life having low to normal blood pressure, then boom out of nowhere you have high blood pressure. In life bad things happen and most of the time it is out of our control. I have noticed that a positive relationship can help calm anxiety and keep your blood pressure in check. Think about it. A negative relationship will do the exact opposite. You could be friends with someone for 20 years but people can still change for better or for worse. Sometimes we have to let go of our childhood friendships for the sake of our wellbeing. You really have to ask yourself if the relationship is worth it.

I have taken my case before Yahweh many times. I have shed tears over lost relationships. I'll admit, giving up a friendship is not as easy as one would think. When we form relationships with people, be around their family, and so on, we tend to create soul ties. A soul tie is a sentimental and spiritual attachment between two people that can be created through various types of relationships, such as romantic, familial, or platonic. Think back to your childhood when you made a good amount of friends and then had to move for some reason. You have to attend a new school, make new friends and this can be challenging for anyone. So, you just lost all of your friends that you knew for years. This is not always easy to accept or deal with. I moved around a lot as a child so I can personally speak on this. See Case Law **§ Psalms 42:11** KJV - "Why art thou cast down, O my soul? and why art thou disquieted within me? hope thou in Yahweh: for I shall yet praise him, who is the health of my countenance, and my Yahweh." Consider this, people who encounter helpful, positive relationships produce more oxytocin and are less likely to fall victim to the adverse effects of stress, anxiety, and grief. Stay far away from people who tend to drain you, put you down, and ultimately want to see you fail.

Yahweh wants us to be in relationships that will help us thrive. You deserve to be happy. I deserve to be happy. We all deserve to be happy, end of story. See Case Law **§ Proverbs 16:20** KJV - "He that handleth a matter wisely shall find good: and whoso trusteth in the LORD Yahweh, happy is he." We must be strong when the time comes to let go of matters that are no longer working in our favor. It is challenging to move on from a past relationship or attachment, even when it's no longer healthy or helpful. Countless times I have wasted and lost from toxic friendships. I am sure you have had similar experiences, if not worse. You most likely experienced similar dreams, coincidences, or a sense of knowing what the other person is thinking or feeling without a word being said. This and more, are all considered soul ties. This could contribute as to why we cannot let go. If you want to live a long, peaceful, loving, and productive life, you must let go of the things and people that mean you no good. See Case Law **§ Deuteronomy 33:29** KJV - **"**Happy art thou, O Israel: who is like unto thee, O people saved by the LORD Yahweh, the shield of thy help, and who is the sword of thy excellency! and thine enemies shall be found liars unto thee; and thou shalt tread upon their high places." Your health matters, never forget that.

We must stay energetic and lively by exercising and eating right. The encouragement of a good friend could give you the needed support to stay on track. Adhering to Yahweh's dietary laws is a perfect way to keep your health in check and stay spiritually well. Afterall, you are what you eat! The dietary laws of Yahweh are found in the book of Leviticus chapter 11 KJV. For example, see Case Law **§ Leviticus 11:47** KJV - "To make a difference between the unclean and the clean, and between the beast that may be eaten and the beast that may not be eaten." What we put in our bodies plays a role in how we feel, act, and think. Being in a healthy relationship causes your brain to release these chemicals: dopamine, adrenaline, and norepinephrine. This makes your heart beat faster and evoke stronger reactions. When we are in good relationships, we feel little to no pain. One can experience true heaven on earth when they are in their own land and home. The same can be said of living in a healthy environment. See Case Law **§ Micah 4:10** KJV - "Be in pain, and labour to bring forth, O daughter of Zion, like a woman in travail: for now shalt thou go forth out of the city, and thou shalt dwell in the field, and thou shalt go even to Babylon; there shalt thou be delivered; there the LORD Yahweh shall redeem thee from the hand of thine enemies."

Love is the most powerful force you can experience. Love trumps hatred. Love removes all negative aspects present in one's circumference. Being in a loving relationship makes you happy and it allows you to be healthy. See Case Law **§ 1 John 4:16** KJV - "And we have known and believed the love that Yahweh hath to us. Yahweh is love; and he that dwelleth in love dwelleth in Yahweh, and Yahweh in him." When we have healthy relationships, they could potentially help keep us free from disease. Let's not forget, a healthy lifestyle also plays a role in how we feel. Exercising is good for your health overall. Eating healthy foods also help keep you in a good mood and it helps you live longer. We know that every relationship is not perfect but that does not mean we should not try to improve it. A healthy relationship should consist of characteristics that will bring about positive outcomes for everyone. Do you trust your friend or partner? Do you have mutual respect for each other? Are you able to be yourself around them? Lastly, are you honest and open with one another? There are other factors that could be taken into account but we will stick with just these for now. Not having all of your needs met in a relationship can have negative effects on your health.

See Case Law **§ Song of Solomon 8:7** KJV - "Many waters cannot quench love, neither can the floods drown it: if a man would give all the substance of his house for love, it would utterly be contemned." A key component of a healthy relationship is trust. If you cannot trust an individual, you will likely bring unnecessary stress on yourself. Constantly worrying about whether someone is being truthful to you is a headache alone. See Case Law **§ Psalms 118:8** KJV - "It is better to trust in the LORD Yahweh than to put confidence in man." An unstable relationship is vile. Do everything in your power to steer clear of these types of situations. Anything out of your control is out of your control. Leave it be. Do not try and force a relationship especially when the end results in you getting hurt. What's even worse is that an undependable so-called friend should never earn the title of friend. They are not your friend. This can harm your self-confidence and future relationships dealing with an undependable person. They are selfish and you will be crestfallen. Focus on relationships that will help keep you sane. Relationships are meant to be a give and take type of relationship, a healthy one anyway. You should give a little and you should take a little. They should give a little and they should take a little too.

You cannot just take and take and expect the recipient to keep putting up with you. Patience truly is a virtue. I can admit that I have to work on being more patient. We all have something about ourselves that we must work on. Life is about growth and with growth comes change. See Case Law **§ 1 John 4:20** KJV - "If a man say, I love Yahweh, and hateth his brother, he is a liar: for he that loveth not his brother whom he hath seen, how can he love Yahweh whom he hath not seen". Time allows healing. Because of time, I was able to preserve some of my relationships. Sometimes we need a break from one another. Separation is a way of healing in its own unique way. When we separate ourselves from destructive relationships, this allows us to get some of our strength back. Some will only heal by letting that relationship go entirely. Some of us do not want to let go of long-term relationships, which actually hinders us from growth. Relationships aren't the only factors that could affect your health. A job could take a toll on your health as well. I know from personal experience how much a job can impact your health. Just know that if your place of employment is bringing illness into your life, it may be time to leave that job and find something else.

You cannot place a price on peace of mind. Pay up or get caught up. See Case Law

**§ Psalms 91:2** KJV - "I will say of the LORD Yahweh, He is my refuge and my

fortress: my Yahweh; in him will I trust." It is true, Yahweh will never let you

down nor leave you in distress. I want to testify to you today that Yahweh is the

Almighty CREATOR and there is no else! It can be a challenge when you cannot

be yourself around someone you consider a friend. Not only will you be

uncomfortable, you are living a lie. How can you flourish as an individual if you

have to live a lie? I have personally witnessed people who lie to one another, call

each other up only to keep tabs on what the other is doing. Who wants to live like

this? I cut people out of my life once I become aware of this type of behavior. I do

not want to be friends with anyone if every word out of their mouth is a lie. What's

the point? Why be fake friends? Can you imagine the toll it could take on your

health? See Case Law **§ Hebrews 13:18** KJV - "Pray for us: for we trust we have a

good conscience, in all things willing to live honestly." It is reasonable that we

should take good care of ourselves. Your well-being is of utmost importance. A

sound relationship is a goal we must keep in mind. Being sound ourselves,

provides us with the confidence we need to go out and take on the world.

Being free from error, fallacy, or misapprehension allows us to give sound advice in our relationships. When you are in excellent health, it will show through good judgment or sense. See Case Law **§ Proverbs 3:5** KJV - "Trust in the LORD Yahweh with all thine heart; and lean not unto thine own understanding." Maintaining your health allows you to be free of wounds or injuries. There's nothing like feeling restored! To be mentally or emotionally sound is to experience wholeness. Generally in the beginning of a relationship, people tend to hold back and exercise caution about what they're willing to reveal. Some people never drop their guard. Ever. See Case Law **§ Psalms 62:8** KJV - "Trust in him at all times; ye people, pour out your heart before him: Yahweh is a refuge for us. Selah." The life we have been blessed with is priceless. We all have different needs, and boundaries exist for a reason. No one wants something forced upon them. Forcing your beliefs, methods, or thought process onto another individual could backfire greatly. It is also detrimental to one's health. Having boundaries does not mean you have to be secretive. My husband lets me do so much until he cannot take it anymore. I let him do so much until I cannot take it anymore.

See Case Law **§ 1 Timothy 4:10** KJV - "For therefore we both labour and suffer reproach, because we trust in the living Yahweh, who is the Saviour of all men, specially of those that believe." Healthy boundaries vary from person to person. You must identify what you both will and will not accept in your dealings.

See Case Law **§ Psalms 40:4** KJV - "Blessed is that man that maketh the LORD Yahweh his trust, and respecteth not the proud, nor such as turn aside to lies." An obsessive or toxic relationship might manifest as someone demanding to know where someone else is or what they're doing at all times. Talk about a headache! If something or someone radiates toxicity, stay away from it or them. Your health can take a dive when someone demeans or belittles you. With that being said, it would be wise to only deal with or involve yourself with others who have a mutual respect for you. It's common sense that respect is something we expect. Unfortunately, not everyone does this. No one has the right to make you feel low in character, status, or reputation. We should build each other up not tear each other down. It's not right when someone wants to cause you to turn aside or away from what is good or true or morally right. This definitely is not good for your health.

See Case Law **§ Deuteronomy 16:19** KJV - "Thou shalt not wrest judgment; thou shalt not respect persons, neither take a gift: for a gift doth blind the eyes of the wise, and pervert the words of the righteous." When we are righteous and work to make the world a better place, our health improves. We cannot allow one bad appleseed to cause us to turn aside or away from what is generally done or accepted. I know how good it feels to do the right thing. When your health starts to fade, it can cause you to divert to a wrong end or purpose and ultimately cause you to make bad decisions. Just like a bribe, you will inevitably twist the meaning or sense of the situation, whatever it may be. Never allow yourself to weaken the morale you stand for. See Case Law **§ Acts 13:10** KJV - "And said, O full of all subtilty and all mischief, thou child of the devil, thou enemy of all righteousness, wilt thou not cease to pervert the right ways of the Lord Yahweh?" Do not throw yourself into disorder because of bad people or situations. When we speak ill of something, it can have negative impacts on our health. Thus, we must speak positively even when it is difficult. Yes, this can be very challenging and is easier said than done. Do not allow anyone to corrupt your way of thinking or being.

There are individuals in this world who thrive off of corruption and believe me, their reign is coming to an end. People are tired of endless wars, hunger, murder, theft, and so on. There are enough good people in the world to replace the bad ones. With Yahweh's help, nothing is impossible. A world without peace takes a toll on your health. It's not healthy to be restless. How can someone get a good night's sleep when people are wreaking havoc relentlessly? See Case Law **§ 1 Kings 3:14** KJV - "And if thou wilt walk in my ways, to keep my statutes and my commandments, as thy father David did walk, then I will lengthen thy days." If you lessen your morals, you not only place little value on yourself, but you take away the dignity that you once had. Relationships that are lower in grade, rank, or status is a no- no. Why degrade yourself? Our minds already play tricks on us enough as it is. If you do not keep your mind at work in a positive way, you will face an uphill battle. Never allow an individual to drag you down in moral or intellectual character. Healthy relationships are defined by love and respect. Align your words with action so you won't lack or decline in good reputation: a state of being held in low esteem. See Case Law **§ Proverbs 14:34** KJV - "Righteousness exalteth a nation: but sin is a reproach to any people."

When we feel good about ourselves, we tend to perform better. Having good communication with people, especially relationships, has its benefits. Remember, our main objective is to maintain healthy relationships that will nurture us. When confrontations arise, those in healthy relationships are able to prevent self-directed attacks. Sometimes discords can be an opportunity to strengthen a relationship with your better half. Healthy relationships are not about keeping score nor feeling that you owe the other soul. We should do things for one another because we genuinely want to. See Case Law **§ Isaiah 51:7** KJV - "Hearken unto me, ye that know righteousness, the people in whose heart is my law; fear ye not the reproach of men, neither be ye afraid of their revilings." Unfortunately, the give and take in a relationship is not always totally equivalent. There are times that one partner may need more help and support than the other. Try your best to keep a positive attitude during these trying times. We also should be cautious not to judge another's situation without knowing all the ins and outs of the situation. Most of us have probably witnessed where one partner may simply prefer to take more of a caregiver role than the other. Such disparity is fine as long as each person is okay with the arrangement.

See Case Law **§ 1 Corinthians 15:33** KJV - "Be not deceived: evil communications corrupt good manners." We must keep in mind that relationships do change over time and not every relationship will be healthy all the time. It is a fact that a relationship is unhealthy when the bad outweighs the good. Again, one must ask themselves if the relationship is worth it. Will you be able to endure and overcome the constant torment from stress? Unacceptable instances like lack of privacy, or being scared to share your opinion, or feeling pressured are signs an individual is feeling or being abused. See Case Law **§ Psalms 125:4** KJV - "Do good, O LORD Yahweh, unto those that be good, and to them that are upright in their hearts." If you are married, unequal control over shared assets such as money or transportation is not a good thing. Someone in the marriage must compromise. If only one person is working, the other should chip in around the house or wherever attention is needed. Maintaining a healthy friendship or marriage takes work. You cannot be the only one who is trying to make things better. This kind of situation can leave one feeling stressed, angry, and emotionally drained. Everyone must be willing to do their part to preserve the relationship and workout any issues that may exist. Make a vow to each other that you'll do the task to build a stronger union.

See Case Law § **Titus 3:8** KJV - "This is a faithful saying, and these things I will that thou affirm constantly, that they which have believed in Yahweh might be careful to maintain good works. These things are good and profitable unto men." It's a good gesture when you can show just how much you appreciate your relationship. This will definitely help to improve the health of any relationship and your well-being. Even when you feel you are giving more than you are receiving, Yahweh will bless you when you least expect it. The ultimate relationship to have is with Yahweh. He is the ultimate healer. He can work miracles. And Yahweh is your best friend. See Case Law § **Psalms 147:3** KJV - "He healeth the broken in heart, and bindeth up their wounds." You will not have any bumps in the road with Yahweh. When we take out time and learn from him, we gain a sound mind. There is no way to have any problems because He solves them. We can always make room to grow our relationship with Yahweh. There is no limit. Every chance I get to learn something new about Yahweh, I take it. It will take a lifetime to study your name, the bible, history etc. So, we should make an effort to learn all that we can about Yahweh; His laws, statues, judgements and commandments. This will prolong your life as it allows healing.

See Case Law § **Deuteronomy 8:3** KJV - "And he humbled thee, and suffered thee to hunger, and fed thee with manna, which thou knewest not, neither did thy fathers know; that he might make thee know that man doth not live by bread only, but by every *word* that proceedeth out of the mouth of the LORD Yahweh doth man live."

For Yahweh gives us our health, our breath, our livelihood, and so much more. Thus, Yahweh is the ultimate healer and friend.

# Chapter 7

It is wise to put all of your trust in Yahweh, for He truly is our friend. See Case Law **§ Ecclesiasticus 6:7** KJV - "If thou wouldest get a friend, prove him first and be not hasty to credit him." Many of us are quick to throw that title "friend" to people just because we've dealt with them for some time or even grew up with them. The fact of the matter is that we truly do not know people like we think we do. People can switch up on you at the flip of a dime. But Yahweh remains the same and unchanged. See Case Law **§ Malachi 3:6** KJV - "For I am the LORD Yahweh, I change not; therefore ye sons of Jacob are not consumed." Some people grow up with siblings they think they know, but their siblings turn out to be complete strangers to them in the end. We must test the spirit of a person. Time will tell where each of us stand. We can truly rely on Yahweh. You have to ask yourself, can you truly rely on this so-called friend? Do they have your best interest at heart? Do they give you sound advice?

When you speak to them about your concerns, are they truly listening? Feedback from a person will tell you all you need to know. Does this so-called friend put you down or make you feel bad on a regular basis? If so, something important is lacking in your relationship. Some people pretend to be your friend until they get tired or no longer want to talk. Ever had a friend that kept in touch but it was only just to keep tabs on you? I call people like that close watchers. You should not have to change who you are just because someone else makes you feel unworthy. We all have different skill sets, ideas, thoughts, and unique qualities. A real friend will help you become better in many ways for your own benefit and not just theirs. When I look in the mirror, I always ask Yahweh to help mold me into the woman he wants me to be. I know Yahweh is the Almighty Creator and the only one able to do this. See Case Law **§ Proverbs 3:7** KJV - "Be not wise in thine own eyes: fear the LORD Yahweh, and depart from evil." When I speak to the people that I consider genuine friends, I am always complimenting them. I try to give them words of encouragement. I do tell them that Yahweh will always be a better friend to them than I could ever be because it is true. At first, I never even thought to utter words like that out of my mouth.

It was when I learned that Yahweh truly is our friend that I felt the need to let others know this. This very thought inspired me to write this book. I want the world to know the truth, that they truly do have a friend indeed, our heavenly father, Yahweh. How many people do you know that have revealed to you that Yahweh truly is your only friend? How many times have you been informed that Yahweh will be a better friend to you than them? I will share with you that none of my friends have ever said this to me. It does not mean my friends are not good people. Yahweh reveals certain things to a few of us. It is up to us whether we want to share that information or not. I am choosing to share this knowledge to help people gain a better understanding of just how important it is that they build a relationship with Yahweh more so than man. Yahweh will always be there for us and how many of us can say that about our friends? Time allows change and thus, people can change. See Case Law **§ James 4:4** KJV - "Ye adulterers and adulteresses, know ye not that the friendship of the world is enmity with Yahweh? whosoever therefore will be a friend of the world is the enemy of Yahweh." A real friend is someone you can trust to tell you the truth and keep their word.

Don't get me wrong, Yahweh has barak (blessed) some of us to have real genuine friends in our lives. It's the ones who behave opposite of what a friend is that we have to be on the lookout for. Another sign a so-called friend is not trustworthy is if they often promise you things or say they will do something and it does not get done. There have been many instances when I have asked a so-called friend to help me with something and they rarely come through. I have asked for copies of documents, links to certain internet sites, et cetera and I never hear back from them. Some people would probably remind them but I feel that if I am your friend it should be important enough for you to remember. It can be difficult to have faith in people at times because of these experiences. We should do our best to treat one another as we want to be treated. Keeping your word was paramount back in the day, or in biblical times. See Case Law **§ Deuteronomy 23:23** KJV - "That which is gone out of thy lips thou shalt keep and perform; even a freewill offering, according as thou hast vowed unto the LORD Yahweh thy God, which thou hast promised with thy mouth." Also, consider see Case Law **§ 1 John 2:5** KJV - "But whoso keepeth his word, in him verily is the love of Yahweh perfected: hereby know we that we are in him."

In my lifetime I admit that I was not always a good friend. I had to learn how to become a good friend. I looked up the definition of "friend" and its characteristics. This allowed me to adjust my behavior, shift my thoughts, and turn words into action. Friends share personal information about themselves with one another. This is about each of you opening up about the private parts of your lives and your feelings towards each other. See Case Law **§ James 2:23** KJV - "And the scripture was fulfilled which saith, Abraham believed Yahweh, and it was imputed unto him for righteousness: and he was called the Friend of Yahweh." If you open up to one another, it means you both trust and value your friendship. There have been times when I apologized to a friend of mine. In past times, I did not always do what was right and I could have made better choices in how I handled a matter. I am grateful that time allows both healing and transformation. There was a time where I told my friend that I could have been a better friend to them in their time of need. We do not always make the right choice, especially when we are young. When you know better, you most likely will do better. Only someone who cares about your feelings will make an effort to make you feel good and sufficient around them.

Our feelings are important and carry weight. We all matter. We should not ignore how we feel. It's important that we all feel good about ourselves. A real friend knows this and will carry themselves like so. Real friends go out of their way to make you feel good and be happy. When my friends would come into town, I would ask them what they wanted to do. It brings me joy to see them enjoying themselves. It just feels good to do good for others. This is what Yahweh teaches us to do. See Case Law **§ Luke 6:38** KJV - "Give, and it shall be given unto you; good measure, pressed down, and shaken together, and running over, shall men give into your bosom. For with the same measure that ye mete withal it shall be measured to you again." Halleluyahweh for the truth! We have absolutely no reason to be greedy, selfish, or mean to one another. Yahweh is our sole provider and He is our friend. When you're in a rough spot, a true friend will be there to help you. Some people are pure at heart and will help you even if they do not consider you as a friend. I thank Yahweh for all the good and righteous people on the Earth. Yahweh is a true friend who always has your back. May we continue to learn from Yahweh through the good book known as our Holy Bible. We can all learn from each other if we take the time to listen and consider each matter at hand.

You must exercise caution before giving someone the title "friend" at the end of the day. Let us strive to become better individuals so that we can become better friends to others. May Yahweh be with us all, and may He continue to be our navigator in this mysterious concept we call life. Shalom Aleichem.

# References

1. *The Holy Bible, King James Version*. Cambridge Edition: 1769; *King James Bible Online*, 2024. www.kingjamesbibleonline.org.

2. *Merriam-Webster Dictionary*. An Encyclopedia Britannica Company Online, 2024. www.https://www.merriam-webster.com.

3. *Oxford English Dictionary*. (2024). "Relationship." in the Oxford English Dictionary online. Retrieved from https://www.oed.com.

4. King James Version with Apocrypha, American Edition (KJVAAE): King James Version 1611, spelling, punctuation and text formatting modernized by ABS in 1962; typesetting © 2010 American Bible Society. Online 2024. https://www.bible.com/bible/546/GEN.1.KJVAAE.

5. Strong, James. *The New Strong's Expanded Exhaustive Concordance of the Bible*. Red letter ed., online. Thomas Nelson, 2022. Retrieved from https://strongsconcordance.org/. Site design and coding © copyright 2022, Danny Carlton Strong's Exhaustive Concordance of the Bible is public domain.

# About Me

Tamar Israel is an author dedicated to spreading the knowledge of Yahweh. She has written transformative works such as יהוה Knowledge of Equity and The Laws of יהוה, designed to guide readers toward just judgments and alignment with the 613 laws, statutes, judgments, and commandments Yahweh has instructed us to follow.

Her books serve as roadmaps for living a life of purpose, fulfillment, and enlightenment in a chaotic and confusing world.

Born in the Nation of Yahweh in Miami, Florida, Tamar was honored to be named by Yahweh Ben Yahweh and attended private school at Yahweh's Educational Center (YEC). Inspired by the desire to help others avoid unintentionally breaking Yahweh's laws, Tamar's first book was created as a study tool focused exclusively on these divine principles. Her works are unique, blending nonfiction with esoteric insights and offering a fresh perspective on timeless truths.

Tamar attended The Art Institute of Philadelphia for Computer Animation and has been a licensed Notary Public for over 19 years. With more than 17 years of experience in the healthcare industry, she continues to work while raising four beautiful children with her husband.

Tamar's books reflect her deep passion for guiding others to live in harmony with the universal laws that connect us all.

If you're interested in learning more about Tamar and her works, please visit her at the following website online www.lulu.com/spotlight/iamtamarisrael.com.